Spelling Success

CLASS 4

Peter Clutterbuck

Blake
EDUCATION
Better ways to learn

To Jessie O'Brien

Spelling Success Class 4

Published by Scholastic India Pvt. Ltd.
A-27, Ground Floor, Sigma Centre
Infocity-1, Sector 34, Gurgaon-122001 (India)
Info-in@scholastic.asia

Author: Peter Clutterbuck
Editor: Kerry Davies
Cover and internal design: Janice Bowles
Typesetter: Julian Mole, Post Pre Press.

ISBN: 978-93-5471-823-6
First edition 2010
This reprint edition: June 2024
Printed in India

Contents

Term 1

✓ Tick when completed

Unit	Phonological Knowledge	
1	Long a sound patterns	☐
2	Short a sound patternss	☐
3	Long e sound patterns	☐
4	Short e sound patterns	☐
5	Long i sound patterns	☐
6	Short i sound patterns	☐
7	Revision	☐
8	Test 1	☐
9	Test 2	☐
	Word Function Knowledge	
10	Plurals, adding s or changing the spelling	☐
11	Plurals, adding es	☐
12	Plurals, words ending in y	☐
13	Plurals, words ending in f or fe	☐
14	Revision	☐
15	Test	☐
	Meaning Knowledge	
16	Compound words 1	☐
17	Compound words 2	☐
	Word History Knowledge	
18	Root words	☐

Term 2

✓ Tick when completed

Unit	Phonological Knowledge	
19	Long o sound patterns	☐
20	Short o sound patterns	☐
21	Long u sound patterns	☐
22	Short u sound patterns	☐
23	r-Influenced vowels, ar and or	☐
24	r-Influenced vowels, er, ir and ur	☐
25	Revision	☐
26	Test 1	☐
27	Test 2	☐
	Word Function Knowledge	
28	Adding ed or ing, no change	☐
29	Adding ed or ing, doubling letters	☐
30	Adding ed or ing, words ending in e	☐
31	Base words, adding ed	☐
32	Revision	☐
33	Test	☐
	Meaning Knowledge	
34	Homophones 1	☐
35	Homophones 2	☐
	Word History Knowledge	
36	Food names	☐

Contents continued

Term 3

✓ Tick when completed

Unit	Phonological Knowledge
37	Sound patterns, aw and au
38	Sound patterns, ee and oo
39	Sound patterns, oa, oi and oy
40	Sound patterns, ai and ie
41	Sound patterns, ea
42	Sound patterns, ow
43	Revision
44	Test 1
45	Test 2

	Word Function Knowledge
46	Base words, adding ing
47	Suffixes, ly
48	Word endings 1
49	Word endings 2
50	Revision
51	Test

	Meaning Knowledge
52	Homographs
53	Anagrams

	Word History Knowledge
54	Shortened words

Term 4

✓ Tick when completed

Unit	Phonological Knowledge
55	Sound patterns, ou
56	Sound patterns, ch and sh
57	Sound patterns, th and wh
58	Sound patterns, ck and qu
59	Consonant blends
60	Silent letters
61	Revision
62	Test 1
63	Test 2

	Word Function Knowledge
64	Comparisons, no change
65	Comparisons, changing spelling
66	Prefixes
67	Possessives
68	Revision
69	Test

	Meaning Knowledge
70	Contractions
71	Tricky words

	Word History Knowledge
72	What do they mean?

	Book 4 Review and Tests
73	Review
74	Test 1
75	Test 2
76	Test 3

Page	Appendixes
77	Useful Words
78	WINK: Words I Need to Know
79	Some Tips for Learning to Spell
80	Assessment
81	Glossary of Terms

About This Book

The *Spelling Success* series provides students with learning activities that embrace the different elements of the spelling system. Each book focuses on the different scope and sequences in the development of spelling skills for each age group or skill level.

These books are not a complete spelling course in themselves, neither are they meant to be, but they provide both students and teachers with the content needed to produce best practices in spelling.

The activities in each book are sequential through the four terms of the school year. This means that it's best to start at the beginning of the Term 1 section and work though to the end, before commencing Term 2 activities, and so on. There are 76 units in this book, 18 per term plus four Review and Test units. Each term is divided into the four areas of knowledge that need to be understood and learned in order to develop a comprehensive mastery of spelling:

Phonological Knowledge — how words sound

Word Function Knowledge — how word function can change spelling

Meaning Knowledge — how context can change word form

Word History Knowledge — how words have been derived

The Phonological Knowledge and the Word Function Knowledge sections include Revision and Test sheets for each term. Four units of Review and Test sheets covering the whole book are provided at the end of Term 4.

This book also contains useful tools to support students with their spelling. At the back of the book you'll find:

- ★ Useful Words list
- ★ WINK: Words I Need to Know — space to record problematic words
- ★ Some Tips for Learning to Spell
- ★ Assessment checklist
- ★ Glossary of Terms

Answers to all activities are provided in a special liftout section. A useful **topic list** for the whole year is given before the units.

Spelling Success provides an integrated method of teaching phonics, spelling and vocabulary. These books will improve literacy skills through effective instruction and evaluation based on the latest research into how spelling is best taught and learned successfully.

Book 4 Topic Chart

TOPIC	UNIT
Adding ed or ing, doubling letters	29
Adding ed or ing, no change	28
Adding ed or ing, words ending in e	30
Anagrams	53
Base words, adding ed	31
Base words, adding ing	46
Comparisons, changing spelling	65
Comparisons, no change	64
Compound words	16,17
Consonant blends	59
Contractions	70
Food names	36
Homographs	52
Homophones	34,35
Long a sound patterns	1
Long e sound patterns	3
Long i sound patterns	5
Long o sound patterns	19
Long u sound patterns	21
Plurals, adding es	11
Plurals, adding s or changing the spelling	10
Plurals, words ending in f or fe	13
Plurals, words ending in y	12
Possessives	67

TOPIC	UNIT
Prefixes	66
r-Influenced vowels, ar and or	23
r-Influenced vowels, er, ir and ur	24
Revision	13
Root words	18
Short a sound patternss	2
Short e sound patterns	4
Short i sound patterns	6
Short o sound patterns	20
Short u sound patterns	22
Shortened words	54
Silent letters	60
Sound patterns, ai and ie	40
Sound patterns, aw and au	37
Sound patterns, ch and sh	56
Sound patterns, ck and qu	58
Sound patterns, ea	41
Sound patterns, ee and oo	38
Sound patterns, oa, oi and oy	39
Sound patterns, ou	55
Sound patterns, ow	42
Sound patterns, th and wh	57
Suffixes, ly	47
Tricky words	71
What do they mean?	72
Word endings	48,49

Long a sound patterns

The letter a is sometimes pronounced as a long a sound, as in **baby** and **whale**.

A Write each word from the box in its correct sentence below.

lazy	**fatal**	**vacant**	**bracelet**	**escape**
bacon	**crater**	**crayons**	**behave**	**waste**

1. We ate ______________ and eggs for breakfast.
2. After we cleaned the classroom we put the ______________ paper bin out.
3. She wore a pretty gold ______________ around her wrist.
4. There was a ______________ accident at the crossroads.
5. Josh is a very ______________ student and never helps anyone else.
6. The derelict building is now ______________ and will be demolished.
7. The prisoner tried desperately to ______________ from the cell.
8. The teacher was sure we would all ______________ correctly on the excursion.
9. I coloured in the picture with my ______________.
10. The scientist walked around the ______________ of the volcano.

B Find all the long a words in the grid and write them beside their meanings.

s	t	a	b	l	e	s
f	a	m	o	u	s	p
d	c	r	a	n	e	i
a	c	h	a	s	e	r
i	w	h	a	l	e	a
s	d	r	a	k	e	t
y	b	l	a	d	e	e
r	a	i	n	b	o	w

1. lifting machine ______________
2. to go after ______________
3. well known ______________
4. large ocean mammal ______________
5. flower ______________
6. male duck ______________
7. cutting part of a knife ______________
8. sea robber ______________
9. horses' homes ______________
10. colourful prism ______________

Parent/Teacher Signature Date

UNIT 2

Short a sound patterns

Sometimes the letter a is pronounced as a short a sound, as in **bat** and **apple**.

A Find the short a sounding words in the grid and write each beside its meaning.

x	c	a	m	e	l	g	v
x	a	t	t	i	c	a	a
c	a	n	v	a	s	l	n
t	a	b	l	e	t	l	i
c	a	c	t	u	s	o	s
p	l	a	n	e	t	p	h

1. desert plant ______________
2. disappear ______________
3. top room of a house ______________
4. animal with a hump ______________
5. thick strong cloth ______________
6 movement of a horse ______________
7. medicine pill ______________
8. heavenly body ______________

B Write each short a word from the box beside a word it can be linked to in some way below.

tadpole	**traffic**	**palace**	**lantern**	**cabbage**
hammer	**magic**	**wagon**	**chapter**	**nappy**

1. nail ______________
2. cars, trucks ______________
3. king ______________
4. lettuce ______________
5. frog ______________
6. wand ______________
7. wheel ______________
8. book ______________
9. baby ______________
10. torch ______________

C Write the words from the box under their headings below.

habit **maybe** **cabin** **cable** **layer** **rapid** **change** **batter**

Long a words		**Short a words**	
______________	______________	______________	______________
______________	______________	______________	______________

Parent/Teacher Signature Date

Long e sound patterns

The letter e can be pronounced as a long e sound, as in **neon** and **female**.

A Write each long e word from the box in its correct sentence below.

fever	**even**	**here**	**these**	**compete**
female	**cedar**	**evening**	**meter**	**complete**

1. A male pig is a boar, while a ______________ pig is called a sow.
2. The numbers five and seven are odd while two and four are ______________.
3. We waited until it cooled down in the ______________ before going outside.
4. The two schools are going to ______________ against each other in sport.
5. The workers hope to ______________ the new road by May.
6. In our garden is a water ______________ that tells how much water we use.
7. The man called his two dogs to come ______________.
8. Isabelle is quite ill as she has a ______________.
9. A large ______________ tree is growing in the backyard.
10. We do not know who ______________ belong to.

B Write each long e word from the box beside a word it can be linked to in some way below.

easy	**neat**	**trapeze**	**beetle**	**canteen**
season	**peanut**	**greedy**	**neon**	**asleep**

1. autumn ______________
2. difficult ______________
3. circus ______________
4. glutton ______________
5. light ______________
6. awake ______________
7. hazelnut ______________
8. untidy ______________
9. food ______________
10. insect ______________

Parent/Teacher Signature Date

UNIT 4

Short e sound patterns

The letter e is sometimes pronounced as a short e sound, as in **bet** and **wet**.

A Find the short e words in the cramped row of words below and write them beside their meanings.

tennisletterinsectpencilcentfencecentresentencetwentypest

1. middle of a circle ________________
2. small amount of money ____________
3. sport ________________
4. six-legged creature ____________
5. writing implement ________________
6. group of words ________________
7. nuisance ________________
8. number ________________
9. border around a home ____________
10. written note ____________

B Add the correct ending from the brackets to these short e word fragments to fit the meanings.

1. met_____	(al, el)	iron, steel
2. lev_____	(al, el)	even, not bumpy
3. den_____	(im, in)	strong cloth
4. lem_____	(in, on)	sour fruit
5. ped_____	(el, al)	part of a bike
6. pet_____	(al, el)	part of a flower
7. med_____	(il, al)	award for bravery
8. nev_____	(ar, er)	not ever
9. sev_____	(en, in)	a number
10. mel_____	(in, on)	fruit from a vine

C Write these short e words in sentences of your own:

dentist ____

clever ____

Parent/Teacher Signature Date

Long i sound patterns

The letter i is sometimes pronounced as a long i sound, as in **hive** and **dive**.

A Write each long i word from the box in its correct sentence below.

pirate	**alive**	**describe**	**iceberg**	**higher**
spider	**surprise**	**driveway**	**ninety**	**blindfold**

1. The ______________ made a large web to catch insects.
2. The police asked her to ______________ the person who stole the watch.
3. We stopped halfway up the mountain but the others went ______________.
4. We put a ______________ on each person to pin the tail on the donkey.
5. The ______________ buried the treasure on a deserted island.
6. We were surprised to find the plants were still ______________ after the frost.
7. We are having concrete laid in our ______________.
8. The ship was lucky not to crash into the large floating ______________.
9. The number that is ten less than one hundred is ______________.
10. We organised a ______________ birthday party for our teacher.

B Complete the long i words below by adding a word ending from the box.

ger	**day**	**ren**	**nus**	**val**
lent	**lot**	**tle**	**dle**	**mare**

1. pi______ (person who flies a plane)
2. Fri______ (day of the week)
3. si______ (alarm)
4. ti______ (striped animal)
5. si______ (noiseless)
6. ti______ (name of a book)
7. mi______ (less)
8. ri______ (competitor)
9. bri______ (harness to guide a horse)
10. night______ (scary dream)

Parent/Teacher Signature Date

UNIT 6

Short i sound patterns

The letter i can also be pronounced as a short i sound, as in **bit** and **sit**.

A Find the short i words in the grid and write them beside their meanings.

d	i	n	n	e	r
c	i	t	y	s	p
k	l	s	c	l	i
i	i	k	h	i	l
t	z	i	i	p	l
t	a	n	l	p	o
e	r	n	l	e	w
n	d	y	y	r	s
w	i	n	t	e	r

1. head rests on a bed _______________
2. a large town _______________
3. a baby cat _______________
4. a reptile _______________
5. cool _______________
6. soft footwear _______________
7. not fat _______________
8. cold season _______________
9. meal of the day _______________

B The underlined words in these sentences are all short i words. Read each one and after each write Yes or No.

1. A severe storm of wind and snow is a blizzard. __________
2. A boy can be your sister. __________
3. A lemon can be quite bitter. __________
4. You wear a mitten on your feet. __________
5. If you turn round and round you could become dizzy. __________
6. In winter the days are always hot. __________
7. Criminals are sometimes put in a prison. __________
8. A mouse is big but an elephant is little. __________
9. You can use a tissue to wipe your nose. __________
10. An insect has ten legs. __________

Parent/Teacher Signature   Date

Revision

A Write the words from the box under their headings below.

apple	crayon	stage	cactus
stable	tadpole	wagon	behave

Long a sound		Short a sound	
____	____	____	____
____	____	____	____

B Write the words from the box under their headings below.

here	tennis	complete	pest
pencil	easy	cent	female

Long e words		Short e words	
____	____	____	____
____	____	____	____

C Write the words from the box under their headings below.

limb	highest	hive	comic
ninety	twist	knit	chime

Long i words		Short i words	
____	____	____	____
____	____	____	____

Parent/Teacher Signature Date

Test 1

The underlined words are spelled wrongly. Write each correctly in the space at the end of the line.

1	The horse was kept in a stabel.	1
2	I have a packet of creyons on my desk.	2
3	This tent is made of canvis.	3
4	We saw the tudpoles in the pool.	4
5	He told the small boy to come heer.	5
6	Did she complet the job?	6
7	She spent ten sents at the shop.	7
8	A beetle is a kind of inset.	8
9	She got a lovely surprize of her birthday.	9
10	The pylot landed the jet on the runway.	10
11	A goanna is a kind of large Australian lisard.	11
12	In winta we go skiing in the snow.	12

Total correct ______ / 12

Parent/Teacher Signature   Date

Test 2

Choose the correct spelling of the word in brackets and write it in the space.

1 The baby was sleeping in a (cradel, cradil, cradle). [ ] 1

2 The film star is very (famous, famos, famus). [ ] 2

3 He packed the (basket, barscet, baskit) full of food. [ ] 3

4 She has lots of (magic, margik, magik) tricks to show us. [ ] 4

5 We took a (deeture, detour, detur) around the highway. [ ] 5

6 I found the work quite (ezy, easy, eezi). [ ] 6

7 Oliver has a very bad (temper, tempa, timper). [ ] 7

8 We were given a friendly (welkum, welcome, welcom). [ ] 8

9 We all appreciated her (kineness, kindness, kindnas) [ ] 9

10 The light is shining (brightly, britely, brigtly). [ ] 10

11 We swam the all the way across the (riva, river, riffer). [ ] 11

12 She showed me the (pictcha, pictoor, picture). [ ] 12

Total correct ______ / 12

Parent/Teacher Signature   Date

UNIT 10

Plurals, adding s or changing the spelling

A Plural means more than one. For many words you simply add s to make their plurals. Examples: one book, two books; one sparrow, several sparrows

Complete each sentence and make the word in brackets mean more than one.

1. We counted ten ________________ flying overhead. (bird)
2. There are six ________________ on the tree. (apple)
3. Several brown ________________ are in the paddock. (cow)
4. I read four ________________ last week. (book)
5. I put all the ________________ in the back room. (chair)
6. Lots of ________________ were growing in the garden. (weed)
7. Charlotte has lots of ________________ to look after. (pet)
8. Mia shared the box of ________________ with me. (pencil)

B To make the plurals of some words you change the way the word looks. Examples: one louse, two lice; one tooth, two teeth

Write the plurals of the words in the boxes.

1.  one man two ________________	**4.**  one mouse four ________________
2.  one foot two ________________	**5.**  one goose two ________________
3.  one woman three ________________	**6.**  one child two ________________

Parent/Teacher Signature Date

Plurals, adding es

A To make the plural (more than one) of many words you need to add es. Some of these are words that end in ch or sh. Examples: one church, two churches; one sash, four sashes

Add es to make each word in the boxes mean more than one.

1.  one watch two ________	**4.**  one peach four ________
2.  one dish several ________	**5.** 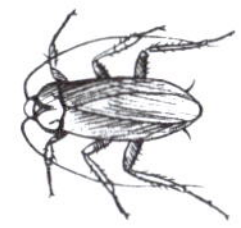 one cockroach lots of ________
3.  one bunch many ________	**6.**  one match two ________

B To make the plural of words that end in s, ss, x or z you also need to add es. Examples: one gas, two gases; one guess, two guesses; one fox, two foxes; one buzz, many buzzes

Complete each sentence below by making the word in brackets mean more than one and writing it in the blank.

1. Lots of ________ bring children to our school. (bus)
2. We saw three ________ last night. (fox)
3. Oxygen and nitrogen are two ________. (gas)
4. I'll give you three ________ to see if you can get it right. (guess)
5. We put the toys in the five cardboard ________. (box)
6. Many of the ________ broke when they fell onto the floor. (glass)
7. This lady has lots of pretty ________. (dress)
8. She could hear all the ________ from the snakes. (hiss)

Parent/Teacher Signature Date

UNIT 12

Plurals, words ending in y

To make the plural (more than one) for some words that end in y after a vowel (a, e, i, o, u) you just add s, as in **one day, two days**. If the word ends in a y after a consonant you need to change the y to an i and then add es, as in **one city, many cities**.

Make each word in the boxes mean more than one .

1. 

one toy two ______________

2. 

one story two ______________

3. 

one baby two ______________

4. 

one turkey three ______________

5. 

one cherry two ______________

6. 

one fly several ______________

7. 

one lady two ______________

8. 

one donkey two ______________

9. 

one key three ______________

10. 

one poppy three ______________

Parent/Teacher Signature Date

Plurals, words ending in f or fe

A For some words that end in f or fe you simply add s to make their plurals. Examples: one gulf, two gulfs; one carafe, two carafes

Add s to make the words in brackets mean more than one and write them in the blanks.

1. The police officer had two pairs of ________________. (handcuff)
2. The ship had to sail between two dangerous ________________. (reef)
3. Snow White is said to have made friends with seven ________________. (dwarf)
4. We saw four ________________ at the zoo. (giraffe)
5. The many ________________ along this coastline bring lots of visitors. (cliff)
6. Ella had a cold so she took two ____________________ to school. (handkerchief)
7. During the storm the ________________ of four houses were blown off. (roof)
8. The farrier had to trim the ________________ of the horses. (hoof)

B To make the plurals of some words that end in f or fe you need to change the f to v and then add es. Examples: one elf, two elves; one life, two lives

Write the plural of the words in the boxes.

1. 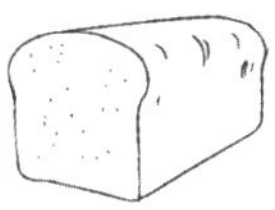 one loaf two ________________	**4.**  one half six ________________
2.  one knife three________________	**5.**  one scarf two ________________
3.  one wolf two ________________	**6.**  one leaf three ________________

Parent/Teacher Signature Date

UNIT 14

Revision

A All the words in the box are singular (one). Turn each one into a plural (more than one) and write it under the correct heading below.

lady	fly	tree	fox
bus	pencil	diary	wish
trolley	poppy	match	key
lolly	dress	paper	city
peach	donkey		

+ s		+ es		Change y to i + es	
______	______	______	______	______	______
______	______	______	______	______	______
______	______	______	______	______	______

B Write the plural of each word in the brackets in the space.

1. The genie gave the girl three ______________. (wish)
2. There are six ______________ in the carpark. (bus)
3. There are three football ______________ on today. (match)
4. I saw lots of ______________ at the farm. (turkey)
5. Melbourne and Sydney are two large ______________. (city)
6. The dentist extracted three of his ______________. (tooth)
7. There were three ______________ in the gymnasium. (woman)
8. The cat caught six ______________ yesterday. (mouse)

Parent/Teacher Signature Date

Test

The underlined words are spelled wrongly. Write them correctly in the spaces.

1	Oxygen and nitrogen are both important <u>gasses</u>.	1
2	Sophie has lots of <u>dreses</u> to wear.	2
3	We saw lots of <u>donkies</u> at the farm.	3
4	My father breeds lots of <u>parrotes</u>.	4
5	Tom ate two <u>peachs</u> for his lunch.	5
6	We saw lots of <u>fairys</u> in the movie.	6
7	I put the three drinking <u>glases</u> on the table.	7
8	We saw several <u>giraffs</u> at the zoo.	8
9	I used the two <u>knifes</u> to cut the meat.	9
10	My brother ate the two <u>lollys</u> I'd been keeping.	10
11	Two <u>branchs</u> on the tree broke off.	11
12	Lots of <u>flys</u> landed on the cake.	12

Total correct ______
12

Parent/Teacher Signature   Date

UNIT 16

Compound Words 1

Compound words are two or more words joined together to make one new word. Examples: any + thing = anything; some + where = somewhere

A Complete each compound word below by adding a word from the box.

road	**chair**	**bird**	**fish**
house	**gull**	**brow**	**shoe**

1. lady__________ 2. gold__________ 3. cross__________ 4. arm__________

5. eye__________ 6. horse__________ 7. sea__________ 8. light__________

B Unjumble the letters in brackets to make compound words to match the pictures and write them on the lines.

1.  tug(abot) __________	**4.** 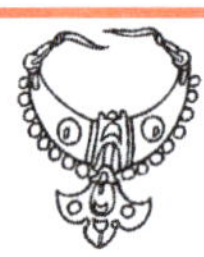 neck(clae) __________	**7.**  camp(rfie) __________
2. 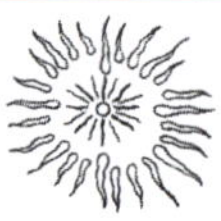 sun(ghlit) __________	**5.**  rain(wbo) __________	**8.**  table(thclo) __________
3.  straw(rreby) __________	**6.** 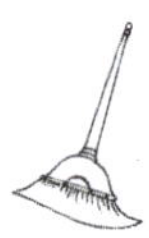 broom(kcist) __________	**9.**  water(llfa) __________

Parent/Teacher Signature Date

Compound Words 2

Compound words are two or more words joined together to make a single word. Examples: rain + bow = rainbow; day + break = daybreak

A Use a word from the box to complete each compound word below.

coat	**ball**	**mill**	**paste**
way	**fish**	**ship**	**hopper**

1. tooth__________ 2. wind__________ 3. foot__________ 4. over__________

5. star__________ 6. space__________ 7. grass__________ 8. free__________

B Add one word from the box in front of each word in the groups below to make compound words.

life	**rain**	**black**	**bed**
home	**horse**	**eye**	**birth**

1.	**2.**	**3.**	**4.**
__________smith	__________room	__________boat	__________coat
__________bird	__________spread	__________jacket	__________drop
__________berry	__________time	__________time	__________fall
5.	**6.**	**7.**	**8.**
__________lash	__________sick	__________day	__________shoe
__________lid	__________made	__________mark	__________back
__________ball	__________work	__________stone	__________power

Parent/Teacher Signature Date

UNIT 18

Root words

Many words we use today have come from the languages spoken by people in the past. These ancient words are called root words.

The following is a list of some of these root words, along with their meanings. Beside each write the word from the boxes below that you think would have come from that root word. Try to think of some more words that could have come from the same root word and write them on the lines below the words. Use a dictionary to help.

1. bindan (to bind) ______________	5. altus (high) ______________
2. wegan (to move) ______________	6. dentis (tooth) ______________
3. mitto (I send) ______________	7. aqua (water) ______________
4. skopeo (I see) ______________	8. pedis (foot) ______________

pedestrian ______________ ______________ ______________	bandage ______________ ______________ ______________
dentist ______________ ______________ ______________	aquarium ______________ ______________ ______________
altar ______________ ______________ ______________	wagon ______________ ______________ ______________
missile ______________ ______________ ______________	telescope ______________ ______________ ______________

Parent/Teacher Signature Date

Long o sound patterns

A The letter o can be pronounced as a long o sound, as in **pony** and **close**.
Choose a word from the box to complete each sentence.

doze
pony
sofa
grocery
hoping
stone
ocean
poem
froze
toe

1. We saw several large cargo ships on the ______________.
2. Chloe wrote a short ______________ about her school.
3. Sophie put a saddle on the ______________ before riding it.
4. I am really ______________ she wins this event.
5. We bought some butter at the ______________ shop.
6. The water in the pipes ______________ during the frosty night.
7. My ______________ ached when the large person stood on it.
8. I was so tired I went to sleep on the ______________.
9. The cruel boy threw a large ______________ at the young magpie.
10. If I lie down after lunch I begin to ______________ off.

B When the letter e is added to the end of a word that has a short o sound, such as **hop**, the sound becomes a long o, as in **hope**.
Write each o + e word from the box beside the word it can be linked to below.

home	**nose**	**alone**	**explode**	**bone**
cone	**rose**	**telephone**	**hotel**	**rope**

1. string ______________
2. daisy ______________
3. smell ______________
4. house ______________
5. ice-cream ______________
6. crowded ______________
7. bomb ______________
8. motel ______________
9. skeleton ______________
10. email ______________

Parent/Teacher Signature Date

UNIT 20

Short o sound patterns

The letter **o** is often pronounced as a short **o** sound, as in **broth** and **shock**.

A Write each word from the box in its correct sentence below.

foggy	cottage	popcorn	doctor	honest
follow	cotton	bottle	blossom	comet

1. The astronomers followed the path of the _______________ using a telescope.
2. The hunting dog began to _______________ the scent of the fox.
3. In the forest there was a small red brick _______________.
4. At the movies I ate some _______________ during the interval.
5. When she was feeling ill Mia decided to see a _______________.
6. Our teacher has told us that it is wise to always be _______________.
7. We sewed the patch on with strong black _______________.
8. The _______________ of soda was put in the refrigerator.
9. The _______________ of the trees had a lovely smell.
10. In winter the mornings are sometimes cold and _______________.

B The short **o** words in these sentences are underlined. Read each sentence and after each write Yes or No.

1. A spider can make a <u>cobweb</u>. _______________
2. A <u>robin</u> is a kind of large animal with a trunk. _______________
3. You should always keep a <u>promise</u>. _______________
4. An ogre is a large mythical <u>monster</u>. _______________
5. You see a <u>comma</u> in the sky at night. _______________
6. A sword is a <u>modern</u> weapon used by soldiers today. _______________
7. We can keep clothes in a <u>closet</u>. _______________
8. If something is <u>common</u> it must be very rare. _______________
9. A <u>novel</u> is a kind of story. _______________
10. If you make a big <u>profit</u> you have lost a lot of money. _______________

Parent/Teacher Signature   Date

UNIT 21

Long u sound patterns

The letter **u** is sometimes pronounced as a long **u** sound, as in **cute** and **huge**.

A Write each long u word from the box in its correct sentence.

pupil	1. The boy made up a clever ______________ for not doing the work.
student	2. These apples taste ______________.
pure	3. The doctor examined the ______________ of her eye.
cubes	4. The ______________ was sorry for what she had done.
music	5. We put the ice ______________ in the glass of lemonade.
fuse	6. The ______________ from the chemical made us feel sick.
mule	7. The ring was made from ______________ gold.
fumes	8. We listened to the ______________ played by the orchestra.
excuse	9. We changed the electrical ______________ when the lights went out.
beautiful	10. A ______________ can be a very stubborn animal.

B Write the long u words that have been cramped up beside their meaning below.

buglepunyreducecutetunastudenttulipperfumestupidcomputer

1. a kind of flower ______________
2. appealing ______________
3. a kind of ocean fish ______________
4. to make less ______________
5. a musical instrument ______________
6. a school pupil ______________
7. sweet scent ______________
8. scraggly ______________
9. a word processor ______________
10. not clever ______________

C Write these long u words in sentences of your own:

useful ____

future ____

Parent/Teacher Signature Date

UNIT 22

Short u sound patterns

The letter u can also be pronounced as a short u sound, as in **cut** and **butter**.

A Find the short u words in the grid and write each beside its meaning.

t	r	u	m	p	e	t	x
t	b	u	t	t	e	r	h
u	b	u	c	k	e	t	u
n	p	u	p	p	e	t	n
n	f	u	n	n	y	x	g
e	u	m	p	i	r	e	r
l	s	u	p	p	e	r	y
t	h	u	n	d	e	r	x

1. noise during a storm ______________
2. amusing ______________
3. referee ______________
4. an evening meal ______________
5. a food made from milk ______________
6. a wooden doll on strings ______________
7. a long hollow in the ground ______________
8. in need of food ______________
9. musical instrument ______________
10. water container ______________

B Find the short u words that have been jumbled up and write each beside a word it can be linked to in some way below.

crustbunchlunchplumuncleuglytruckskullbunkhump

1. camel ______________
2. breakfast ______________
3. aunt ______________
4. pretty ______________
5. bread ______________
6. head ______________
7. bed ______________
8. car ______________
9. fruit ______________
10. banana ______________

C Write these short u words in sentences of your own:

must ______________________________

stump ______________________________

Parent/Teacher Signature   Date

r-Influenced vowels, ar and or

When the letter a is followed by the letter r it changes to a long ar sound, as in **dark** and **park**. When the letter o is followed by the letter r it changes to a long or sound, as in **pork** and **before**. These are called r-influenced vowels.

A Choose the correct ar word from the brackets and write it on the line.

1. When I was fishing in the sea I saw a (shark, park). ________________
2. The third month of the year is (March, Starch). ________________
3. We watched the funny (carpets, cartoons) on television. ________________
4. She grows lots of roses in her (pardon, garden). ________________
5. If you do not eat food you will (starve, carve). ________________
6. He fired and got a bullseye on the (market, target). ________________
7. The new student is very (smart, tart). ________________
8. When it is ripe we (harvest, garden) the crop. ________________
9. When the fire (army, alarm) sounded we left the room. ________________
10. I received a large (parcel, pardon) in the mail. ________________

B Find the or words in this cramped-up list and write each beside its meaning below.

fortycornerstormthorntorchshoreshortstorestorytorn

1. shop ________________
2. number ________________
3. where two walls meet ________________
4. wild weather ________________
5. prickle ________________
6. where sea and land meet ________________
7. tale ________________
8. a light ________________
9. ripped ________________
10. not tall ________________

Parent/Teacher Signature Date

r-Influenced vowels, er, ir and ur

When the letters e, i or u are followed by the letter r they change to a long er sound, as in **stern** and **person**, **stir** and **fir**, **curd** and **spur**. These are called r-influenced vowels.

A Join the word pieces from the box to the spaces below. Each word you make has the letters er.

tim	news	sil	whis	ti	spi

1. ______paper we read it each day
2. ______per to talk quietly
3. ______ger large striped cat
4. ______ber wood for building
5. ______ver a precious metal
6. ______der eight-legged creature

B Write each ir word from the box in its correct sentence below.

circus
circle
smirk
chirp
birthday
squirt
stir
skirt

1. Alice wore a pretty blue ____________ to school.
2. We could hear a small bird ____________ nearby.
3. The principal told her to wipe the ____________ off her face.
4. It will be my tenth ____________ next Monday.
5. I told the boy not to ____________ me with the water pistol.
6. Most of all I enjoyed the clowns at the ____________.
7. Joe drew a large ____________ in his workbook.
8. To the flour you add milk and eggs and then ____________ it well.

C Circle the correct ur word from the brackets.

1. If you blow up a balloon in may (burst, disturb).
2. If you stay in the hot sun you could get (suburb, sunburned).
3. We can boil water in an (urn, turn).
4. A (purse, nurse) is a hospital worker.

Parent/Teacher Signature Date

Revision

A Write the words from the box under their headings below.

ocean	doctor	explode	comet
cottage	cone	cotton	pony

Long o sound ______ ______ ______ ______

Short o sound ______ ______ ______ ______

B Write the words from the box under their headings below.

tulip	bucket	skull	truck
bunch	bugle	music	cube

Long u words ______ ______ ______ ______

Short u words ______ ______ ______ ______

C Write the words from the box under their headings below.

circle	forty	turkey	carton	thorn
ladder	spider	barge	shirt	burst

ar sound	or sound	er sound	ir = er sound	ur = er sound
______	______	______	______	______
______	______	______	______	______

Parent/Teacher Signature Date

Test 1

Choose the correct spelling of the word in brackets.
Write it in the space.

1 We had a swim in the (oshun, ocean, ocune). [ ] 1

2 I spoke on the (telefone, telephone, telaphone). [ ] 2

3 We tried to (follow, fellow, folla) the older boys. [ ] 3

4 I sewed on the patch with (coton, cotten, cotton). [ ] 4

5 We made an (eccuse, excoos, excuse) for being late. [ ] 5

6 Chloe is a (student, studant, studdent) at our school. [ ] 6

7 We filled the (bucet, buckit, bucket) with water. [ ] 7

8 My friend made a (puppit, puppet, pupet) out of paper. [ ] 8

9 It is Sophie's (turn, tern, tirn) to bat. [ ] 9

10 We planted vegetables in the (garden, gardan, gaden). [ ] 10

11 This ring is made of solid (silvar, silver, silva). [ ] 11

12 She felt (thirsty, thersty, thursty) after the run. [ ] 12

Total correct ______
12

Parent/Teacher Signature Date

Test 2

Find the word in each line that is incorrectly spelled.
Write the word correctly in the space.

1	I am hopeing she will come soon.	1
2	Jack was left all aloan when the others went.	2
3	My docktor told me to take these tablets.	3
4	I filled the glass bottil with lemonade.	4
5	What excoose did she give you for being late?	5
6	Josh is a new stewdent in our year.	6
7	I thought the joke he told was very funi.	7
8	I cut the krust off the loaf of bread.	8
9	I saw a sharck at the beach.	9
10	I will meet you at the cawner of the two streets.	10
11	You need to ster the cocoa well to make it dissolve.	11
12	I walked all around my suberb yesterday.	12

Total correct ______ / 12

Parent/Teacher Signature　　　　Date

UNIT 28

Adding ed or ing, no change

We often add ed or ing to the ends of words to make sure they fit correctly into the meaning of a sentence. With many words there is no other change to the spelling.

A Add ed to the word in brackets and complete each sentence.

1. We ______________ everywhere but couldn't find the lost puppy. (look)
2. Cooper ______________ me his new bicycle. (show)
3. We ______________ lots of games this morning. (play)
4. The large jet ______________ at the airport. (land)
5. The frightened children ______________ into the room. (rush)
6. We ______________ as the rabbits ate the lettuce. (watch)
7. I ______________ Will to help me clean the room. (ask)
8. Last week we ______________ in a motel in Melbourne. (stay)
9. Sam and his family ______________ some friends today. (visit)
10. Mia ______________ the children while their mother was shopping. (mind)

B Add ing to the incomplete words and then draw a picture for each one.

1. Sophie is sweep_____ the floor.	**2.** Josh is wash_____ the clothes.	**3.** Jack is cook_____ the meals.
4. Ella is climb_____ the tree.	**5.** Lily is brush_____ the horse.	**6.** Oliver is drink_____ the soda.

Parent/Teacher Signature Date

UNIT 29

Adding ed or ing, doubling letters

When you add ed or ing to a word that ends in a short vowel and one consonant, you double the consonant. Example: drop, dropped, dropping

A Add ed to the words in brackets to complete each sentence.

1. The girl ________________ across the road. (hop)
2. Ella ________________ the wood with an axe. (chop)
3. The speeding car ________________ suddenly at the corner. (stop)
4. The lion ________________ its prey into the long grass. (drag)
5. Charlotte ________________ her leg where an ant bit her. (rub)
6. We ________________ when he had finished the song. (clap)
7. The acrobat ________________ over and over. (flip)
8. The shearers ________________ the horses' manes. (clip)
9. He ________________ the pack to his bicycle. (strap)
10. She ________________ the rope tightly so she wouldn't fall. (grip)

B Add ing to each word at the top and write it in the space and then draw a picture for each one. Don't forget to double the last letter.

1. swim Ethan is ________________ across the pool.	**2.** shop Mia is ________________ in the supermarket.	**3.** run Tom is ________________ across the ground.
4. hit Jack is ________________ the ball.	**5.** cut Emily is ________________ the bread.	**6.** swap The boys are ________________ their marbles.

Parent/Teacher Signature Date

UNIT 30

Adding ed or ing, words ending in e

With words that end in a silent e you drop the e before adding ed or ing. Example: ice, iced, icing

A Add ed to the word in brackets. Complete each sentence.

1. The cat ______________ the mouse. (chase)
2. The dog ______________ the boy from drowning. (save)
3. Sam ______________ his dirty clothes. (change)
4. The cook ______________ some cakes. (bake)
5. The girls ______________ to their friends. (wave)
6. We ______________ the goods in the box. (place)
7. The boys ______________ away from the girls. (race)
8. Ella ______________ into the pool. (dive)
9. I ______________ she would arrive soon. (hope)
10. All the children ______________ the other way. (face)

B Make the words at the top end in ing and write them in the spaces. Then draw a picture for each one.

1. ride	**2.** skate	**3.** bite
Riley is ______________ a horse.	Tilley is ______________ on the ice.	The dog is ______________ the stranger.
4. make	**5.** drive	**6.** hide
Jo is ______________ a box.	Mr Smith is ______________ his new car.	The boys are ______________ in the bushes.

Parent/Teacher Signature   Date

Base words, adding ed

Base words are the words that are used to make other words by adding a suffix like ed.
Example: trick + ed = tricked

A Write the base word that each word comes from.

1. batted comes from ______________
2. washed comes from ______________
3. picked comes from ______________
4. rowed comes from ______________
5. lifted comes from ______________
6. asked comes from ______________
7. pulled comes from ______________
8. covered comes from ______________
9. barked comes from ______________
10. kicked comes from ______________

B Write the base word that each word comes from.

1. dragged comes from ______________
2. chopped comes from ______________
3. rubbed comes from ______________
4. stopped comes from ______________
5. dropped comes from ______________
6. shopped comes from ______________
7. netted comes from ______________
8. called comes from ______________
9. gripped comes from ______________
10. strapped comes from ______________

C Make these words end in ed and write them in sentences of your own. Don't forget to double the last letter.

1. clap ______________________________
2. slap ______________________________
3. drip ______________________________

Parent/Teacher Signature Date

Revision

A Make the words from the box end in ed and sort them under their headings below.

play	skip	fill	hop
step	help	chop	wash
drag	kick	growl	cook
shop	clap	mop	plant

No change		Double last letter	
______	______	______	______
______	______	______	______
______	______	______	______
______	______	______	______

B Make the words from the box end in ing and sort them under their headings below.

block	skip	ride	cook
run	hike	growl	step
skate	help	mop	move

No change	Double last letter	Drop e
______	______	______
______	______	______
______	______	______
______	______	______

Parent/Teacher Signature Date

Test

Choose the correct spelling of the word in brackets.
Write the correct spelling in the space.

1	I (helped, helpt) her remove the rubbish.	1
2	Sophie is (skiping, skipping) across the yard.	2
3	Jack (pickt, picked) all the flowers.	3
4	Shona is (rideing, riding) her bike.	4
5	We are (shoping, shopping) in the supermarket.	5
6	Tom is (swimming, swiming) across the pool.	6
7	The boys are (drinkeing, drinking) the water.	7
8	The tall mountains (blocked, blockt) their way.	8
9	I (asked, ascked) if I could come.	9
10	The horse (troted, trotted) across the paddock.	10
11	Isabella is (scrubing, scrubbing) the floor.	11
12	The boys are (raceing, racing) down the street.	12

Total correct ______
12

Parent/Teacher Signature

Date

UNIT 34

Homophones 1

Homophones are words that sound the same but have different spellings and different meanings. Examples: bear (animal), bare (without covering); sun (star), son (male child)

A Write the word that matches the picture.

1. sail sale  ________	**2.** creak creek  ________	**3.** tow toe  ________	**4.** ate eight  ________
5. flour flower  ________	**6.** rain rein  ________	**7.** knot not  ________	**8.** plain plane  ________

B Find the pairs of homophones in this list of cramped words and write them together.

sumringholerosehourtoewringroarrowstowbluebleworwholerawsome

1. ______ ______ 2. ______ ______ 3. ______ ______ 4. ______ ______

5. ______ ______ 6. ______ ______ 7. ______ ______ 8. ______ ______

C Think of a word that matches each picture. Each word sounds the same as the words below but has a different spelling and a different meaning. Write the new word on the line.

1.  pair ________	**2.**  rows ________	**3.** **72 + 36 = 108** some ________

Parent/Teacher Signature Date

Homophones 2

Homophones are words that sound the same but have different spellings and different meanings. Examples: bear (animal), bare (without covering); sun (star), son (male child)

A Choose the correct word from the box to fill the spaces below.

week	**stake**	**tide**	**cheap**	**stair**
weak	**steak**	**tied**	**cheep**	**stare**

1. I ate a tender piece of ______________ for tea.
2. When it was trapped the moose was ______________ up with rope.
3. It will be at least a ______________ before the parcel arrives.
4. It is rude to ______________ at people.
5. These shoes I bought were quite ______________.
6. We could not go fishing because the ______________ had gone out.
7. The gardener hammered in a ______________ to keep the plants erect.
8. The lady felt hungry and ______________ after being lost in the bush.
9. I climbed up the ______________ to my classroom.
10. We could hear the soft ______________ of the new chick.

B Unjumble the letters of the homophones in brackets. Write each one on the line.

1. ate (geiht)	**2.** plain (lpane)	**3.** been (eban)	**4.** rein (arin)
______________	______________	______________	______________
5. pair (rpea)	**6.** male (amil)	**7.** rode (orad)	**8.** hoarse (ohrse)
______________	______________	______________	______________

Parent/Teacher Signature Date

Food names

Many words we use have their origin (where they came from) in ancient languages, such as Old English and Latin (the language of the ancient Romans), or from other modern languages, such as French.
The word **bread** comes from an Old English word meaning **fragment**. The word **pumpkin** comes from a Greek word meaning **ripen in the sun**.

A By research, try to find out how these foods were named. Use a dictionary to help.

1. spaghetti ______________________
2. corn ______________________
3. date ______________________
4. lettuce ______________________
5. cabbage ______________________
6. omelette ______________________

B The word **muscle** comes from a Latin word meaning **mouse**. The Romans had great imaginations didn't they?
Write a non-rhyming poem that compares body parts to animals. Example: My toe is just like a tadpole.

My ____________ is just like a ____________.

My ____________ is just like a ____________.

My ____________ is just like a ____________.

My ____________ is just like a ____________.

Parent/Teacher Signature Date

Sound patterns, aw and au

The letters **aw** are pronounced like an **or** sound, as in **jaw** and **claw**. The letters **au** can also make an **or** sound, as in **taut** and **saucer**.

A Write each aw word from the box in its correct sentence.

yawn
jaw
hawk
straw
lawn
drawn
awful
crawl
dawn
bawl

1. When I took away her lollies the youngster began to ______________ loudly.
2. The bales of ______________ were fed to the hungry cattle.
3. Sophie was so tired she began to ______________.
4. The small ______________ hovered above the mice.
5. We sat on the soft grass of our backyard ______________.
6. Jack's ______________ was quite sore from chewing on the hard lollies.
7. The campers decided to leave just after ______________.
8. It was one of the most ______________ things that had happened.
9. The baby began to ______________ only last week.
10. Ruby has ______________ a picture of a dinosaur in her book.

B The au words below are underlined. After each sentence write Yes or No.

1. The leaves fall from trees in autumn. _________
2. A daughter is a male child. _________
3. An author writes stories. _________
4. When you are naughty you behave well. _________
5. You might clean clothes at a laundry. _________
6. We often put sauce on our food. _________
7. We drink coffee from a saucer. _________
8. You would see an audience at a concert. _________

C Write these au words in sentences of your own:

caught ____

automatic ____

Parent/Teacher Signature

Date

UNIT 38

Sound patterns, ee and oo

The letters **ee** together make a long **e** sound, as in **deep** and **peep**. The letters **oo** together can be pronounced in two ways:

(a) a long **oo**, as in **boot** and **scoot**
(b) a short **oo** sound, as in **took** and **rook**.

A Find the **ee** words in the grid and write them beside their meanings below.

c	q	u	e	e	n	f	w
h	c	r	e	e	k	i	h
e	s	w	e	e	t	f	e
e	f	l	e	e	t	t	e
s	k	n	e	e	l	e	l
e	s	t	e	e	l	e	s
a	s	l	e	e	p	n	x

1. building material from iron ______________
2. group of ships ______________
3. to bend on one knee ______________
4. small stream ______________
5. royal family member ______________
6. food made from milk ______________
7. not sour ______________
8. not awake ______________
9. number ______________
10. there are four on a car ______________

B Fill in the missing letters to make a long **oo** word to match each picture.

1.  h______ves	**2.**  sn______ze	**3.**  sch______l	**4.**  r______ster
5. 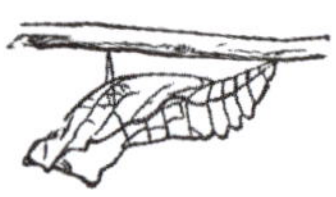 coc______n	**6.**  t______th	**7.**  g______se	**8.** 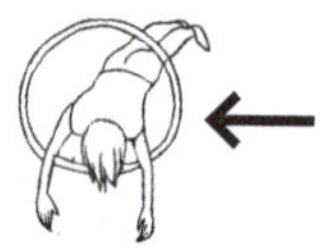 h______p

Parent/Teacher Signature   Date

Sound patterns, oa, oi and oy

A The letters oa together make a long o sound, as in **coat** and **moat**.

Add a word fragment from the box to the spaces below to make a long o word.

oat	oad	oast	oat	oaves
oast	oak	oach	coa	oak

1. b_____ (brag about yourself)
2. t_____ (breakfast food)
3. thr_____ (part of your neck)
4. t_____ (a frog-like creature)
5. cl_____ (long draping clothing)
6. s_____ (to thoroughly wet through)
7. m_____ (water around a castle)
8. l_____ (how bread is baked)
9. c_____ (to train people in a sport)
10. co_____ (chocolate drink)

B The letters oi or oy together are pronounced as an oy sound, as in **moist** and **hoist**, **toy** and **coy**.

Write each oi or oy word from the box in its correct sentence below.

choice
joint
moist
poison
spoiled
voice
noise
annoy
enjoy
loyal

1. We were not allowed to make a _____________ in the library.
2. Lachlan's dog is faithful and _____________.
3. Don't drink that liquid as it may be a kind of _____________.
4. Because she talked a lot Mia's _____________ was often hoarse.
5. The blowflies began to _____________ the picnickers.
6. The knee is a _____________ of your leg.
7. I always _____________ watching the cartoons on television.
8. Sophie had to make a _____________ between swimming and shopping.
9. These towels are dry but this one is still quite _____________.
10. The rancid sauce _____________ the taste of our meal.

Parent/Teacher Signature Date

Sound patterns, ai and ie

A The letters ai together are often pronounced as a long a sound, as in **bait** and **mail**.

Find the ai words in the grid. Write them beside a word they can be linked to in some way below.

s	t	r	a	i	g	h	t
s	g	r	a	i	n	a	d
a	c	h	a	i	n	f	r
i	d	a	i	s	y	r	a
l	t	r	a	i	n	a	i
o	s	n	a	i	l	i	n
r	p	a	i	n	t	d	s

1. shell ____________
2. flower ____________
3. links ____________
4. wheat ____________
5. crooked ____________
6. ship ____________
7. water ____________
8. scared ____________
9. brush ____________
10. carriage ____________

B The letters ie together can make two different sounds:
(a) a long e sound, as in **piece** and **thief**
(b) a long i sound, as in **pie** and **die**.

Find the ie words in the grid and write them beside their meanings.

t	n	i	e	c	e	d	b
h	g	r	i	e	f	i	r
i	d	r	i	e	d	e	i
e	c	r	i	e	d	d	e
f	f	r	i	e	d	x	f

1. cooked in oil ____________
2. sadness ____________
3. female relation ____________
4. to have passed away ____________
5. to have wept tears ____________
6. without any water ____________
7. short ____________
8. robber ____________

Parent/Teacher Signature Date

Sound patterns, ea

The letters ea together can be pronounced in two different ways:
(a) a long e sound, as in **beat** and **east**
(b) a short e sound, as in **thread** and **head**.

A Each ea word in the box has a long e sound. Write each beside its meaning below.

leaf	**stream**	**clean**	**beam**	**leap**
peach	**wheat**	**cream**	**beach**	**steal**

1. cereal ______________
2. type of stone fruit ______________
3. part of a tree ______________
4. ray of light ______________
5. take secretly ______________
6. not dirty ______________
7. fat part of milk ______________
8. sandy shore of the sea ______________
9. jump ______________
10. river or creek ______________

B Each ea word in the box has a short e sound. Write each in its correct sentence.

feathers	1. We were not quite sure what he ______________.
bread	2. He stopped running to catch his ______________.
head	3. We are going swimming ______________ of playing cricket.
instead	4. This weight is very ______________ to lift.
leather	5. The ______________ I ate for lunch had poppy seeds in it.
meant	6. Birds like to keep their ______________ clean.
weather	7. When he walked into the door he hurt his ______________.
ready	8. These shoes are made of fine ______________.
heavy	9. Our football team is really ______________ for the match.
breath	10. The ______________ has been cold and rainy lately.

Parent/Teacher Signature Date

UNIT 42

Sound patterns, ow

The letters ow together can be pronounced in two ways: (a) an ow sound as in **how** and **cow** (b) a long o sound, as in **tow** and **low**.

A Find the ow words in the grid and write each beside its meaning below.

c	r	o	w	n	x	x
p	f	l	o	w	e	r
o	b	a	c	c	t	t
w	r	l	l	r	o	o
d	o	l	o	o	w	w
e	w	o	w	w	e	e
r	n	w	n	d	l	r
s	h	o	w	e	r	x

1. a drying cloth ____________
2. a large gathering of people ____________
3. a circus performer ____________
4. a king wears one ____________
5. fine crushed rock ____________
6. it is in your bathroom ____________
7. a colour ____________
8. to let someone do something ____________
9. a tall building ____________
10. the seed-bearing part of a plant ____________

B Each word in the box has the letters ow pronounced as a long o sound. Write each in its correct sentence.

arrow
elbow
mower
hollow
shadow
window
yellow
snowing
shallow
pillow

1. We cut the long grass with the ____________.
2. We painted the house dark blue and ____________.
3. The bright sun created a large ____________ under the tree.
4. I put the ____________ on my bed to rest my head.
5. The bow and ____________ are on the table.
6. When I woke up cold I saw it had been ____________.
7. This end of the pool is deep but the other end is ____________.
8. Your ____________ is a joint of your arm.
9. This tube is solid but those over there are ____________.
10. I opened the ____________ to let in some fresh air.

Parent/Teacher Signature Date

Revision

A Add the sound units aw or au to complete each word.

1. d______ghter (female child)
2. d______n (daybreak)
3. s______cer (holder for a cup)
4. h______k (small bird of prey)
5. l______n (grassy area)
6. n______ghty (to misbehave)
7. b______l (cry loudly)
8. s______ce (we pour it on food)

B Add the sound units ee or oo (as a long o sound, as in **boot**, or a short o sound, as in **look**) to complete each word.

1. sn______ze (sleep)
2. fl______t (group of ships)
3. fift______n (a number)
4. r______ster (male chook)
5. kn______l (bend on one knee)
6. g______se (farmyard bird)
7. cr______k (small stream)
8. sch______l (place of education)

C Add the sound units oa or oi to complete each word.

1. l______f (slab of bread)
2. m______st (damp)
3. t______st (a breakfast item)
4. j______nt (your knee or elbow)
5. c______st (land meeting the ocean)
6. p______son (dangerous substance)
7. sp______led (ruined)
8. t______d (creature like a frog)

D Write the ea words from the box under their headings below.

feather	**ready**	**beach**	**bread**
stream	**cream**	**breath**	**steal**

ea = long e sound ______ ______ ______ ______

ea = short e sound ______ ______ ______ ______

Parent/Teacher Signature Date

Test 1

Choose the correct spelling of the word in brackets. Write the correct word in the space.

1	When his head hit the wall the boy hurt his (jor, jaw).	1
2	Mr Smith's (dorter, daughter) is a pharmacist.	2
3	We left the camp at (dorn, dawn).	3
4	I often put tomato (sorce, sauce) on my food.	4
5	The (queen, quene) was sitting on the throne.	5
6	The (wheel, weel) on the car was damaged.	6
7	I had a short (snuze, snooze) after school.	7
8	The (ruster, rooster) was with the hens.	8
9	We rowed the (bowt, boat) across the water.	9
10	I cooked some (toste, toast) for my breakfast.	10
11	Don't drink that because it may be (poison, poisin).	11
12	Her (voice, voise) was quite hoarse.	12

Total correct ______
12

Parent/Teacher Signature   Date

Test 2

Choose the correct sound unit to complete each word.

1 The baby began to cr____l at six months of age. (au, aw)

2 The farmer harvested the oats and wh____t in summer. (ee, ea)

3 The mouse nibbled the piece of ch____se. (ie, ee)

4 I am in year four at my sch____l. (oo, ee)

5 It is unwise to b____st about your achievements. (or, oa)

6 She had to make an important ch____ce. (oy, oi)

7 There was a t____er in the middle of the city. (ow, ou)

8 I did not know what our teacher really m____nt. (ie, ea)

9 The water ran out of the dr____n. (ay, ai)

10 The speech she gave was quite br____f. (ee, ie)

11 When we finish mopping the floor the kitchen will be cl____n. (ee, ea)

12 This box of toys is quite h____vy (ee, ea)

Total correct ______ / 12

Parent/Teacher Signature Date

Base words, adding ing

A base word is a word that is used to make other words by adding a suffix like ing.
Example: plant + ing = planting

A Write the base word each word is made from. The first one has been done for you.

1. feeling comes from *feel*
2. weeping comes from ______________
3. helping comes from ______________
4. picking comes from ______________
5. weeding comes from ______________
6. climbing comes from ______________
7. drinking comes from ______________
8. asking comes from ______________
9. pulling comes from ______________
10. rowing comes from ______________

B Write the base word each word is made from. The first one has been done for you.

1. clapping comes from *clap*
2. mopping comes from ______________
3. skipping comes from ______________
4. swimming comes from ______________
5. chopping comes from ______________
6. running comes from ______________
7. putting comes from ______________
8. shopping comes from ______________
9. planning comes from ______________
10. digging comes from ______________

C Write the base word each word has been made from. The first one has been done for you.

1. liking comes from *like*
2. taming comes from ______________
3. hiking comes from ______________
4. moving comes from ______________
5. tasting comes from ______________
6. racing comes from ______________
7. skating comes from ______________
8. riding comes from ______________
9. shaping comes from ______________
10. baking comes from ______________

Parent/Teacher Signature Date

Suffixes, ly

The letters ly together form a suffix that is added to the end of a base word to change its meaning.
Example: quiet + ly = quietly

A Make the word in brackets end in ly. The first one has been done for you.

1. The sun was shining ___brightly___. (bright)
2. The boys ran ______________ across the oval. (quick)
3. The small boy faced the bully ______________. (brave)
4. The choir sang the songs ______________. (loud)
5. The snail crawled ______________ across the lettuce. (slow)
6. The new girl did her work ______________. (bad)
7. The young girl sang ______________. (sweet)
8. The girl accepted the award ______________. (proud)
9. They got across the pool ______________. (safe)
10. He avoided his opponent ______________. (clever)

B For words that end in y you change the y to i and then add ly (**lazy** + ly = **lazily**). For some words that end in e you drop the e and then add ly (**idle** + ly = **idly**). For some words that end in e you just add ly, as in **bravely** and **safely**.
Make the words in brackets end in ly and complete these sentences.

1. He sat ______________ in the chair. (comfortable)
2. She tripped and fell ______________. (heavy)
3. She replied ______________ to him. (angry)
4. He ate the cakes ______________. (hungry)
5. They moved from the room ______________. (noisy)
6. She lifted the baby ______________. (gentle)
7. He won the race ______________. (easy)
8. She ______________ enjoyed his company. (true)
9. He was ______________ disappointed. (terrible)
10. It was ______________ the worst day of her life. (possible)

Parent/Teacher Signature   Date

UNIT 48

Word endings 1

Some word endings look and sound similar and so are easily confused. The word endings en, in, on and ain all sound much the same, like an en sound, as in **open**, **cabin**, **dragon** and **captain**. The word endings le and el also look similar and sound the same, as in **turtle** and **travel**.

A Add the correct word ending, en, in, on or ain, in the space. The first one has been done for you.

1. There are sev__en__ dogs in the kennel.
2. She wore a red ribb______ around her head.
3. My cous______ James lives in Adelaide.
4. There is a large fount______ in the middle of the city.
5. She sewed on the patch with some black cott______.
6. We planted some pumpk______ seeds.
7. The glass fell and is now brok______.
8. When I spilled some food I reached for the napk______.
9. We could see the snow-covered mount____ in the distance.

B Use a word from the box to complete each sentence. Each word has either an le or an el ending.

bottle
kettle
travel
camel
little
middle
table
turtle
gravel

1. After it was tarred the workers put ______________ over the road.
2. In the desert a ______________ is a useful animal for carrying cargo.
3. My parents will ______________ to England in a large jet.
4. He pushed a pin through the ______________ of the circle.
5. Ethan helped me move the ______________ to the front of the room.
6. We boiled the ______________ to make a cup of tea.
7. I bought a ______________ of lemonade from the milkbar.
8. An elephant is big but a mouse is ______________.
9. The ______________ pulled its head and legs into the safety of its shell.

Parent/Teacher Signature   Date

Word endings 2

The word endings **ar**, **er** and **or** also look and sound very similar, but it's important to learn which endings belong with which words. These word endings are usually pronounced like an **er** sound, as in **beggar**, **runner** and **tailor**.

A These words end in **ar**, **er** or **or**. Fill in the missing letters to make a word that matches each picture.

1.  s_____lor	**2.**  an_____or	**3.** 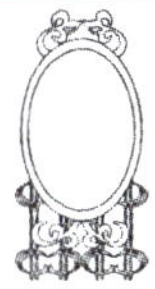 m_____ror	**4.**  l_____der
5.  fr_____zer	**6.**  d_____lar	**7.**  b_____lar	**8.**  tr_____tor

B Add **ar**, **er** or **or** to complete each word below. Use a dictionary if you need to.

1. I tightened the coll_____ on my puppy.
2. Tom is a fast_____ runner than Josh.
3. Mia had a painful blist_____ on her heel.
4. The old cell_____ was very spooky.
5. Our house has sol_____ power.
6. The auth_____ of this book lives in Darwin.
7. The doct_____ listened to my heartbeat.
8. The may_____ of our city owns a furniture shop.
9. We listened to an interesting speak_____ at the assembly.
10. The jogg_____ ran through the city park.

Parent/Teacher Signature Date

UNIT 50

Revision

A Complete the words in the box by adding ar, er or or. Write them under their headings below.

may____	ladd____	doll____	mot____	begg____	mirr____
timb____	sol____		coll____	skat____	regul____
lun____	anch____	tract____	prop____	auth____	

+ ar	+ er	+ or

B Complete these words by adding en, in, on or ain. Write them under their headings below.

capt____	heav____	childr____	brok____
apr____	ribb____	fount____	pumpk____
cab____	curt____	napk____	cott____
elev____	cous____	drag____	mount____

+ en	+ in	+ on	+ ain

Parent/Teacher Signature Date

Test

The underlined words are spelled wrongly. Write them correctly in the spaces.

1	I drank all the water in the bottel.	1
2	The glass fell and is now brokin.	2
3	She replied angryly to the stranger.	3
4	She lifted the baby gentley.	4
5	The keeper is tameing the wild cat.	5
6	The bushwalkers went hikeing up the hill.	6
7	He got safly across the freeway.	7
8	I am going to travle to Germany next year.	8
9	We used some cottin to mend the hole in the cloth.	9
10	There is a tall mountin in this area.	10
11	The farmer used a tracter to plough the fields.	11
12	We have a small turtel in our aquarium.	12

Total correct ______
12

Parent/Teacher Signature

Date

UNIT 52

Homographs

Sometimes two words that have entirely different meanings have exactly the same spelling and are pronounced the same. These are called homographs. Example: box (a container), box (to fight)

A Use each word in the box twice in the sentences below.

train	**rock**	**mine**	**light**	**bear**

1. The stupid boy threw a ______________ at the bird.
2. I cannot ______________ to eat any more of these mushrooms.
3. There used to be a gold ______________ in this area.
4. When I got into bed I switched off the ______________.
5. We travelled to Sydney on an express ______________.
6. Waves can easily ______________ a boat.
7. The large ______________ hunted for salmon in the river.
8. Some swimmers ______________ for their sport every day.
9. Don't touch that as it is ______________ and not yours.
10. These boxes are quite ______________ to lift.

B Circle the descriptions that match the pictures.

1. a creek bank  a bank for money	**2.** to post a letter  a fence post	**3.** the bark of a tree  the bark of a dog
4. a storage box  to box as a sport	**5.** a formal ball  a ball for sport	**6.** a cricket bat 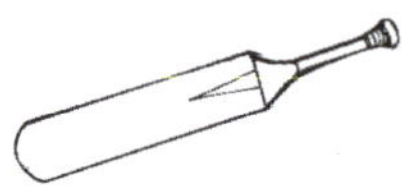 a fruit bat

Parent/Teacher Signature Date

Anagrams

Anagrams are words that contain exactly the same letters as another word or words, but in a different order, as in **dust** and **stud**.

A Rearrange the letters of the words to make another word to match the pictures.

1. lump  ________	**2.** dawn  ________	**3.** lame  ________	**4.** bare  ________
5. grin  ________	**6.** flow  ________	**7.** hose  ________	**8.** reap  ________

B Rearrange the letters of these words to make an anagram of each word. Write the new word in a sentence. The first one has been done for you.

1. lance *I helped my friends clean up the room*
2. sore ________
3. blow ________
4. hoes ________
5. rats ________
6. save ________

Parent/Teacher Signature Date

UNIT 54

Shortened words

Today many words we use have come from much longer words.

Which shortened word we use do you think comes from the word at the top of each box. The pictures will give you a clue.

1. defence

____

2. perambulator

____

3. taximeter cab

____

4. influenza

____

5. periwig

____

6. omnibus

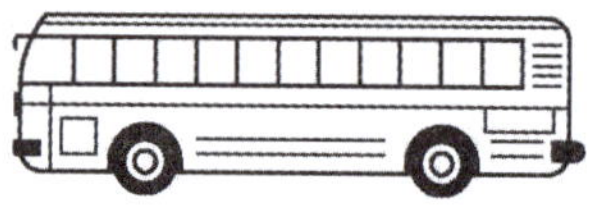

____

7. zoological gardens

____

8. All Hallows Evening

____

Parent/Teacher Signature Date

Sound patterns, ou

The letters **ou** can be pronounced in three different ways: (a) as an **ow** sound, as in **found** and **ground** (b) a long **oo** sound, as in **you** and **wound** (c) a short **u** sound, as in **touch** and **rough**.

A The **ou** words in the box all have the **ow** sound. Use each word in its correct sentence below.

hound	**ground**	**around**	**proud**	**pouch**
found	**thousand**	**flour**	**south**	**outside**

1. The miners ______________ a new reef of gold.
2. The blood ______________ followed the tracks of the convicts.
3. After going east we decided to head ______________.
4. Lachlan fell heavily onto the ______________ and hurt his arm.
5. A kangaroo is an animal that has a ______________ to keep its young.
6. When we finished the test we went ______________ to play.
7. There were over a ______________ people at the concert.
8. We ran ______________ the backyard to get warm.
9. We put the egg whites in with the ______________ and stirred the mixture.
10. My parents were ______________ when I won the race.

B The underlined **ou** words below are pronounced as either the long **oo** sound or the short **u** sound. Answer Yes or No after each sentence.

1. You can have a bowl of <u>soup</u> at meal times. ___________
2. A <u>youth</u> is a very, very old person. ___________
3. It is wise to <u>touch</u> a hot stove. ___________
4. A brave person has a lot of <u>courage</u>. ___________
5. Australia is a tiny <u>country</u>. ___________
6. A deep <u>wound</u> can be very painful. ___________

Parent/Teacher Signature Date

Sound patterns, ch and sh

A The letters ch can represent three different sounds:
(a) ch sound, as in **chop** (b) k sound, as in **chemist**
(c) sh sound, as in **chef**.

Find the ch words in the grid and write each beside its meaning.

c	h	i	c	k	e	n
c	c	h	e	r	r	y
h	c	c	h	e	s	t
e	h	c	h	i	l	d
e	a	c	h	e	s	s
s	s	c	h	i	e	f
e	e	c	h	e	a	p
c	h	a	p	t	e	r

1. food made from milk ______________
2. poultry ______________
3. young person ______________
4. not expensive ______________
5. board game ______________
6. small red fruit ______________
7. leader of a clan ______________
8. to go after to catch ______________
9. part of a book ______________
10. part of your body ______________

B The letters sh are pronounced as in **ship** and **shop**.

Add the word pieces from the box to make words that fit the meanings below.

rimp	**adow**	**iny**	**ampoo**	**oe**
rink	**oulder**	**ovel**	**rub**	**atter**

1. sh________ (small bush)
2. sh________ (part of your body)
3. sh________ (small water creature)
4. sh________ (darkness made by the sun)
5. sh________ (very bright)
6. sh________ (to break into pieces)
7. sh________ (garden tool)
8. sh________ (hair wash)
9. sh________ (footwear)
10. sh________ (to get smaller)

Parent/Teacher Signature Date

Sound patterns, th and wh

A The letters **th** together can make two different sounds: (a) unvoiced, as in **thin** and **thick** (b) voiced, as in **that** and **then**.

All of the words in the box have an unvoiced sound. Write each word in its correct sentence below.

thongs
throat
thunder
thrush
Thursday
throne
threw
thumb
thorn
thirteen

1. Some people think that ____________ is an unlucky number.
2. Cooper ____________ the tennis ball across the yard.
3. He missed the nail with the hammer and instead hit his ____________.
4. Mia wore a pair of ____________ to the beach.
5. The loud ____________ frightened the dogs.
6. The sharp ____________ made his foot bleed.
7. The ____________ built the nest in the ash tree.
8. She has a sore ____________ because she has a cold.
9. The fifth day of the week is ____________.
10. The king sat on his ____________ and spoke to his subjects.

B The letters **wh** together can also represent two sounds: (a) a **w** sound, as in **when** (b) an **h** sound, as in **who**.

Each **wh** word underlined in the sentences below has the **w** sound. Write Yes or No after each sentence.

1. We can make flour from <u>wheat</u>. ________
2. You will find a <u>wheel</u> on a car. ________
3. A <u>whale</u> lives in the desert. ________
4. A zebra is blue and <u>white</u>. ________
5. You might <u>wheeze</u> if you have asthma. ________
6. An umpire blows a <u>whistle</u>. ________

C Write these **wh** words in sentences of your own:

whole ____

whose ____

Parent/Teacher Signature   Date

Sound patterns, ck and qu

A The letters ck together make a k sound (the c is silent), as in **rock** and **sack**.

Find the ck words in the grid and write them beside their meanings.

c	c	r	i	c	k	e	t	p
h	b	u	c	k	e	t	f	a
i	q	u	a	c	k	f	l	c
c	s	t	i	c	k	r	o	k
k	b	r	i	c	k	o	c	e
e	b	l	a	c	k	c	k	t
n	t	h	i	c	k	k	x	x

1. poultry ______________
2. noise of a duck ______________
3. opposite of thin ______________
4. water container ______________
5. dark shade ______________
6. sport ______________
7. piece of wood ______________
8. building block ______________
9. a group of sheep or birds ______________
10. small parcel ______________

B The letter q is almost always followed by a u. It can make two sounds, depending on the vowel sound following:
(a) a kw sound, as in **quack** and **question** (b) a k sound as in **queue**.

Add a word piece from the box to make a qu word that fits the meaning below.

ilt	**ail**	**een**	**eer**	**adrangle**
arry	**arrel**	**artz**	**ince**	**artet**

1. qu________ (an argument)
2. qu________ (small bird)
3. qu________ (ruler)
4. qu________ (odd, strange)
5. qu________ (a four-sided shape)
6. qu________ (bed covering)
7. qu________ (where stone is mined)
8. qu________ (a very hard kind of rock)
9. qu________ (a hard yellow fruit)
10. qu________ (group of four singers)

Parent/Teacher Signature   Date

Consonant blends

Many words begin or end with consonant blends. The letters br (**bread**), cl (**clap**), pr (**price**), and st (**stick**) are common initial consonant blends. The letters mp (**lamp**), nd (**pond**), rt (**part**) and sk (**task**) are common final consonant blends.

A All of the words in the box begin with a blending of two consonants. Write each word beside its meaning below.

clam	**dragon**	**freckle**	**grape**
breakfast	**crayon**	**flour**	**planet**

1. fire-breathing monster ______________
2. writing stick ______________
3. first meal of the day ______________
4. shellfish ______________
5. body that circles the sun ______________
6. a fruit ______________
7. a spot on the skin ______________
8. food made from wheat ______________

B Add a consonant blend from the box to each word fragment below to create a word that matches its meaning.

pr	**scr**	**sp**	**sc**	**sk**	**sn**

1. ____ider (eight-legged creature)
2. ____eam (to yell loudly)
3. ____une (dried plum)
4. ____ooze (to sleep)
5. ____inny (not fat)
6. ____one (type of small bun)

C Add a final consonant blend from the box to complete each word below.

ng	**mp**	**nd**	**st**	**sk**	**nt**	**lt**	**pt**

1. tu____ (horn of an elephant)
2. gue____ (visitor)
3. gru____ (noise of a pig)
4. eucaly____ (gum tree)
5. hou____ (dog)
6. sta____ (used to send a letter)
7. lu____ (breathing organ)
8. adu____ (grown up)

Parent/Teacher Signature Date

UNIT 60

Silent letters

Many words contain letters that you do not sound when saying them aloud, but they must be included when you write them, as for the g in **gnat**, and the final b in **bomb**.

A Write each word from the box beside its meaning below. Circle the silent letters.

crumb	**hour**	**knife**	**palm**	**sword**
limb	**school**	**knee**	**calf**	**wrist**

1. ___________ (place of learning)
2. ___________ (sixty minutes)
3. ___________ (cutting blade)
4. ___________ (joint of the leg)
5. ___________ (joint of the arm)
6. ___________ (tiny scrap of bread)
7. ___________ (arm or leg of the body)
8. ___________ (ancient steel weapon)
9. ___________ (type of tree)
10. ___________ (part of the leg)

B Add the word endings from the box to the spaces below and circle the silent letter in each word.

ost	**gn**	**mb**	**lf**
nest	**eel**	**stle**	**swer**

1. gh___________ 2. an___________ 3. kn___________ 4. ho___________

5. ca___________ 6. si___________ 7. ha___________ 8. bo___________

C Write each of these words in sentences of your own:

wriggle ___________________________

debt ___________________________

knight ___________________________

Parent/Teacher Signature Date

Revision

UNIT 61

A Write the words from the box under the headings below.

bound	around	you	double	touch	cantaloupe
country	soup	group	south	hound	rough

ou = ow sound	ou = long oo sound	ou = short u sound
____________	____________	____________
____________	____________	____________
____________	____________	____________
____________	____________	____________

B Add ch or sh in the spaces to complete each word.

1. ____ampoo (hair soap)
2. ____erry (small red fruit)
3. ____rub (small tree)
4. ____icken (poultry)
5. ____adow (darkness made by the sun)
6. ____riek (to yell loudly)
7. ____ocolate (confectionery)
8. ____isel (carpentry tool)

C Add th or wh to complete each word.

1. ____eat (grain)
2. ____irty (number)
3. ____ite (colour)
4. ____irsty (in need of a drink)
5. ____umb (a digit of your hand)
6. ____ale (ocean mammal)
7. ____isper (talk quietly)
8. ____ief (a person who steals)

Parent/Teacher Signature Date

Test 1

The underlined words are spelled wrongly. Write them correctly on the lines.

1. Be careful not to tuch the hot stove.
2. A kangaroo has a powch for its joey.
3. I had a bowl of soop for lunch.
4. The water is shalo over here
5. This man is the cheef of the workers.
6. He hit his thum with the hammer.
7. All the thick smoke made me weeze.
8. I filled the buket with water.
9. The ducks qacked when I came near.
10. He has lots of fleckles on his face.
11. The gest stayed with us for a week.
12. This pig is fat but that one is scinny.

Total correct ______ / 12

Parent/Teacher Signature　　　Date

Test 2

Choose the correct group of letters to complete the word.

1 The cake is made from eggs, milk and fl____r. (ur, ou, ow))

2 The sandpaper is very r____gh. (oo, ou, ow)

3 She washed her hair with ____ampoo. (ch, sh, th)

4 We got the tablets from the ____emist. (ch, sh, th)

5 The two boys had a ____arrel over the swapcards. (th, qu, ch)

6 I opened the pa____et of seeds. (ck, ch, th)

7 I put an extra ____anket on the bed. (pl, sk, bl)

8 The small ____allow built its nest in the pipe. (st, sw, sl)

9 Will eats too much and is really a ____utton. (gl, gr, bl)

10 This morning I wore my ____ippers for the first time. (sw, st, sl)

11 I am in year four at my s____ool. (sk, ch, th)

12 I filled the ba____et with food. (sh, sk, sp)

Total correct ____ / 12

Parent/Teacher Signature Date

UNIT 64

Comparisons, no spelling change

To compare people or things you can add er or est to describing words. You use er when comparing two people or things and est when comparing three or more people or things. For many words you can add these endings without having to change the way they are spelled.

Example: Sam is **fast**. Jack is **faster** than Sam. Of the three boys Tom is the **fastest**.

A Make each word in brackets end in er. Write the word in the space.

1. Tom is ________________ than Sam. (old)
2. This paper is ________________ than that one. (smooth)
3. A snail is ________________ than a mouse. (slow)
4. This weight is ________________ than a mouse. (light)
5. Tamieka is a ________________ runner than Samantha. (fast)
6. It is much ________________ today than yesterday. (cool)
7. Our classroom is ________________ than that one. (clean)
8. A lion is ________________ than a jackal. (strong)
9. This drink is ________________ than that one. (sweet)
10. My teacher is ________________ than the principal. (young)

B Make the words in brackets end in est.

1. This is the ________________ church in Australia. (old)
2. This is the ________________ room in the school. (clean)
3. Sophie is the ________________ person in my class. (bright)
4. This is the ________________ cliff in these mountains. (steep)
5. This old car is the ________________ in the carpark. (slow)
6. Mia is the ________________ girl in our year. (young)
7. I think Josh is the ________________ boy in our school. (smart)
8. This is the ________________ day we have had all week. (cool)

Parent/Teacher Signature Date

Comparisons, changing spelling

When you add **er** or **est** to a word ending in **y** you change the **y** to **i** and then add **er** or **est**, as in **heavy**, **heavier**, **heaviest**.

If the word ends with a short vowel and then a consonant you double the last letter, as in **hot**, **hotter**, **hottest**.

A Make the word in brackets end in **er**.

1. Oliver is much ________________ than I am. (busy)
2. This desk is ________________ than that one over there. (heavy)
3. An ant is ________________ than a mouse. (tiny)
4. Your class was ________________ than ours when we went to the gym. (noisy)
5. This orchard has ________________ trees than those. (healthy)
6. These turtles are ________________ than those ones. (big)
7. My apple is ________________ than yours. (red)
8. Today is much ________________ than yesterday. (hot)
9. This pig is ________________ than that young one. (fat)
10. These cows are ________________ than those because there is little feed. (thin)

B Complete the chart below by writing in the words.

+ **est**	+ **est**
1. pretty = ________________	6. hot = ________________
2. busy = ________________	7. fat = ________________
3. lucky = ________________	8. mad = ________________
4. heavy = ________________	9. sad = ________________
5. wealthy = ________________	10. fit = ________________

Parent/Teacher Signature Date

UNIT 66

Prefixes

Prefixes are groups of letters added to the beginning of a word to alter its meaning.
Examples: in + visible = invisible (not visible);
re + write = rewrite (write again)

A Add a prefix from the box to the words below. Use each one twice.

in	un	re	mis

1. Lily has promised not to ______behave on the excursion.
2. I am going to ______pay all the money I owe you.
3. The old battered chair was very ______comfortable.
4. These shoes are dear but these are quite ______expensive.
5. Their behaviour was quite ______sensitive.
6. I hope Sophie will ______turn one day.
7. The car has proved to be very ______reliable.
8. She made a big ______take in trusting the new pupil.

B Some prefixes denote a number. Use the prefixes from the box to make a word that matches each picture.

semi = half	uni = one	bi = two	tri = three	quin = five	octo = eight

1.  ______cycle	**2.**  ______tet	**3.**  ______noculars	**4.**  ______circle
5.  ______cycle	**6.**  ______cycle	**7.**  ______pus	**8.**  ______angle

Parent/Teacher Signature Date

Possessives

To show that someone or something owns something, called the possessive, you add an apostrophe and **s** after the word.
Example: The bicycle of the boy. The boy's bicycle.

A Show ownership for the following. The first one has been done for you.

1. the dress of the girl — *the girl's dress*
2. the car of our teacher ____________
3. the pages of a book ____________
4. the howl of the wolf ____________
5. the television of the lady ____________
6. the legs of the chair ____________

B If the word is plural (more than one), you then put the apostrophe after the s. Example: The horns of the cows. The cows' horns.
Rewrite each of these to show ownership. The first one has been done for you.

1. the tails of the dogs
the dogs' tails
2. the manes of the horses
____
3. the roofs of the houses
____
4. the bikes of the boys
____
5. the dresses of the ladies
____
6. the trunks of the trees
____
7. the pens of the teachers
____
8. the hands of the clocks
____

Parent/Teacher Signature   Date

UNIT 68

Revision

A Complete the chart by filling in the spaces to make comparisons. The first one has been done for you.

	+ er	+ est		+ er	+ est
1. slow	*slower*	*slowest*	5. fast	______	______
2. cool	______	______	6. old	______	______
3. clean	______	______	7. steep	______	______
4. young	______	______	8. smooth	______	______

B Complete the chart by filling in the spaces to make comparatisons of these words ending in y. The first one has been done for you.

	+ er	+ est		+ er	+ est
1. busy	*busier*	*busiest*	5. heavy	______	______
2. pretty	______	______	6. tiny	______	______
3. muddy	______	______	7. noisy	______	______
4. dizzy	______	______	8. fussy	______	______

C Add the apostrophe in each word to show ownership.

1. I saw Sams bicycle.
2. We cared for the mans dog.
3. We climbed the cities towers.
4. We looked for a dogs collar.
5. We heard the mouses squeaks.
6. I ironed all the ladies dresses.
7. He raked up the five trees leaves.
8. We cleaned our teachers car.

Parent/Teacher Signature Date

Test

The underlined words are spelled wrongly. Write the correct spellings in the spaces.

1	Today is <u>hoter</u> than yesterday.	1
2	Sam is <u>busyer</u> than Jack.	2
3	A snail is <u>slowar</u> than a dog.	3
4	This is the <u>tinyest</u> insect of all.	4
5	I think Oliver is a lot <u>luckyer</u> than me.	5
6	This apple is <u>reder</u> than the other one.	6
7	This has been the <u>sadest</u> day of my life.	7
8	He rode his <u>trycycle</u> around the block.	8
9	I saw an <u>octapuss</u> at the beach.	9
10	I had to <u>rerite</u> the essay.	10
11	This boy is <u>inreliable</u>.	11
12	When it went into the clouds the jet became <u>unvisible</u>.	12

Total correct ______ / 12

Parent/Teacher Signature   Date

Contractions

A contraction is a shortened form of two words when one or more letters are left out. You use an apostrophe to show where the letters are missing. Examples: is not = isn't; can not = can't

A Write the full words from the box beside their contractions below.

you had	**they are**	**she will**	**I will**	**is not**	**I had**
we had	**she is**	**have not**	**can not**	**did not**	**who is**

1. they're ____________
2. she'll ____________
3. I'll ____________
4. I'd ____________
5. isn't ____________
6. you'd ____________
7. we'd ____________
8. she's ____________
9. haven't ____________
10. can't ____________
11. didn't ____________
12. who's ____________

B Make a contraction of the two words in brackets and then write a sentence using the contraction. The first one has been done for you.

1. (they are) *I think they're going to come later*
2. (we have) ____________
3. (will not) ____________
4. (you have) ____________
5. (I am) ____________
6. (can not) ____________
7. (does not) ____________

Parent/Teacher Signature Date

Tricky words

To spell correctly it is important to know the meanings of words. Because so many words sound and look similar, people often use the wrong word for the meaning of a sentence.

Examples: I have to pairs of shoes. ×
I have two pairs of shoes. ✓
The car is over their. ×
The car is over there. ✓

Write the correct word from the brackets to fill each space. Use a dictionary if you need to.

1. We had a water ______________ installed on our lawn. (metre, meter)
2. The nuts in the wheel became quite ______________. (lose, loose)
3. Although she is short Mia is ______________ a good high jumper. (quite, quiet)
4. I put the clothes in the chest of ______________. (drawers, draws)
5. Everyone ______________ Riley came to my party. (accept, except)
6. The thick smoke made it difficult for us to ______________. (breath, breathe)
7. It is far ______________ cold to go swimming. (too, two)
8. Please put the clothes over ______________. (their, there)
9. Sophie is not ______________ to go. (allowed, aloud)
10. I am sure Chloe ______________ the answer was correct. (knew, new)
11. The fisherman ______________ the boat across the river. (rowed, road)
12. I think ______________ going to help us after all. (there, they're)
13. Will dived ______________ the bridge into the water. (of, off)
14. My parents have decided to ______________ a baby girl. (adopt, adapt)

Parent/Teacher Signature Date

UNIT 72

What do they mean?

A We often use words differently from what they really mean. Write the real meaning of these sayings that have to do with food.

1. That was a very sweet thought.

____

2. You have very good taste in clothes.

____

3. The car we bought was a real lemon.

____

4. The new boy likes to ham it up.

____

5. They were all sandwiched together.

____

B The underlined words all have something to do with animals but they have special meanings in these sentences. Explain what each means.

1. It really bugs me.

____

2. I think there is something fishy about all that.

____

3. I told the children to stop monkeying around.

____

4. I'm going to have a hot dog for lunch.

____

5. The roadmakers are using a bulldozer.

____

Parent/Teacher Signature Date

Revision

A Complete these words to match their meanings and then write them under their headings below.

1. fr_____d (cooked in oil)
2. t_____el (used to dry off)
3. m_____st (damp)
4. cr_____d (wept)
5. t_____st (breakfast food)
6. m_____er (grass cutter)
7. t_____d (frog-like creature)
8. sp_____led (ruined)
9. p_____son (deadly chemical)
10. n_____ce (female relation)
11. cr_____n (royal headwear)
12. shall_____ (not deep)
13. l_____f (slab of bread)
14. br_____f (short)
15. c_____t (clothing)
16. j_____nt (elbow or knee)

oa		oi		ow		ie	
________	________	________	________	________	________	________	________
________	________	________	________	________	________	________	________

B Add **er**, **ir** or **or** in the spaces.

1. Today is his b_____rthday.
2. A large cat is a tig_____.
3. We saw clowns at the c_____cus.
4. I pulled the th_____n out of my finger.
5. Today is hot but yest_____day it was cold.
6. We went to the st_____e to buy some bread.
7. The sand along the sh_____e was a brilliant white.
8. It reached f_____ty degrees during the heat wave.
9. After the long run I felt th_____sty.
10. I climbed a ladd_____ to get onto the roof.

Parent/Teacher Signature Date

Test 1

Choose the correct spelling of the word in brackets. Write each correctly spelled word in the space.

1	We saw three (foxss, foxes) in the bush.	1
2	There were several (gooses, geese) on the farm.	2
3	Sophie has lots of pretty (dresess, dresses).	3
4	On the beach there were two (donkeys, donkies).	4
5	I ate three orange (halfs, halves).	5
6	We saw six (giraffes, giraves) at the zoo.	6
7	There are lots of (flies, flys) in the dish.	7
8	There were five (ladys, ladies) in the room.	8
9	There are two (churches, churchs) in this street.	9
10	I ate all the delicious (berries, berrys).	10
11	Oxygen and nitrogen are both (gases, gasses).	11
12	I stacked all the (bookes, books) on the shelves.	12

Total correct ______
12

Parent/Teacher Signature

Date

Test 2

The underlined words are spelled wrongly. Write them correctly on the lines.

1	The boys are <u>raceing</u> along the street.	1
2	We are <u>moveing</u> to Sydney soon.	2
3	I like to go <u>swiming</u> in summer.	3
4	I am <u>planing</u> to search for the treasure.	4
5	The kangaroo <u>easyly</u> jumped the fence.	5
6	She was <u>truely</u> sorry for what she had done.	6
7	She got across the road <u>safly</u>.	7
8	When it dropped the glass was <u>brokin</u>.	8
9	The workers laid the <u>gravle</u> on the road.	9
10	She wore a red <u>ribben</u> in her hair.	10
11	The ship's captain decided to <u>anchar</u> in the bay.	11
12	The farmer used a <u>tracter</u> to pull the plough.	12

Total correct ______
12

Parent/Teacher Signature   Date

Test 3

Choose the correct spelling of the word in brackets.
Write the correct word on the line.

1	I called a friend on the (telephone, telefone).	1
2	Last night we stayed in a (motel, motle).	2
3	Sam gave his mother a red (toolip, tulip).	3
4	We listened to the pop (musac, music).	4
5	In the army she learned to play a (bugel, bugle).	5
6	He filled the (bottel, bottle) with water.	6
7	A (camle, camel) can go for a long time without water.	7
8	Chloe made a (puppet, pupet) from wood.	8
9	She grows lots of roses in her (gardan, garden).	9
10	Lachlan gave the teacher a bunch of (daisys, daisies).	10
11	This bird has very colourful (fethers, feathers).	11
12	We sewed the patch on with (cotten, cotton).	12

Total correct ______
12

Parent/Teacher Signature Date

Useful Words

account
act
again
almost
alone
also
always
among
another
anyway
April
army
aunt
because
been
before
begin
begun
beside
body
born
both
bought
bridge
broke
brought
build
built
capture
carry
case
caught
cause
centre

chain
change
charge
check
children
church
close
close
collect
complete
contract
copy
country
date
dead
deal
death
December
died
doctor
dollar
done
dozen
dress
drill
driven
early
else
evening
event
except
expect
extra
fair

famous
feel
few
file
fix
flower
follow
four
front
god
goes
great
greedy
ground
happen
hear
heard
heart
held
herself
himself
history
hold
however
income
indeed
inform
inspect
itself
January
know
lead
learn
leased

least
leave
less
list
many
March
matter
mean
meet
member
might
mind
miss
money
month
morning
mountain
need
next
nor
nothing
November
number
October
off
offer
office
omit
once
order
own
paid
pair
past

people
person
picture
plan
please
point
power
press
pretty
prove
provide
push
question
railroad
ready
real
reason
recover
return
road
rule
says
sentence
shall
sight
size
something
sorry
speak
steamer
stole
stood
study
subject

such
suffer
sure
teach
teacher
there
third
those
thought
thus
ticket
tissue
took
trip
true
trust
unable
understand
useful
vanish
vote
were
while
who
wire
wish
within
women
wonder
world
write
wrote
yesterday
young

WINK: Words I Need to Know

For many people, some words are often problematic to spell. Record words you are having difficulty with on this page.

Word	Word	Word

Some Tips for Learning to Spell

★ When you read, look out for the patterns of letters you find in words. Remembering these will help you spell words. For example, these words do not sound the same, but all contain a common letter pattern: cough, rough, through, thought, bough.

★ Take an interest in words, as this is useful in motivating you to persevere with improving your spelling ability.

★ Accept that some difficult words simply have to be learned. A useful strategy for this is the LOOK, COVER, WRITE, CHECK system.

    LOOK at the word and try to form a pattern of the letters in your mind. Ensure you know the meaning of the word and how it is used.

    COVER the word or remove it from your sight.

    WRITE the word from memory.

    CHECK if you are correct.

  If wrong, begin the process again. If right, give yourself a pat on the back.

★ Learn to say words correctly. Many students often have spelling difficulties simply because they pronounce some words incorrectly, and spell them as they think they sound. For example: jumping, not jumpen.

★ Develop the dictionary habit. If you don't know how to spell a word, look it up. Did you know a dictionary is used more for finding the correct spelling of words rather than finding their meanings?

★ Become familiar with the more common rules and guides, and use them.

★ When you are writing and you have guessed the spelling of a word, always check it later.

★ Remember that incorrect spelling is easily noticed by others, so being a good speller can be an aid to employment.

Assessment

	T1	T2	T3	T4
★ Displays an interest in words and their meanings.				
★ Displays an interest in the way the basic sounds of English are used to create words.				
★ Understands that knowledge of sound units assists both reading and spelling development.				
★ Attempts to spell words and makes informed choices with letter sounds and patterns.				
★ Investigates the meanings of words and their special characteristics, such as homophones and compound words.				
★ Readily identifies errors in proofreading activities.				
★ Uses a variety of methods to improve spelling skills.				
★ Utilises memory keys or the LOOK, COVER, WRITE, CHECK method to remember the spelling of difficult words.				
★ Spells at a standard commensurate with chronological age and general educational development.				
★ Reads widely and displays an inherent desire to improve spelling skills.				
★ Takes an interest in all aspects of the classroom program and is prepared to assist others.				

Comments

Teacher

____

____

Student

____

____

Glossary of Terms

adjective
A word that describes nouns or other words.
Examples: **gold** (noun), **golden** (adjective)
wool (noun), **woollen** (adjective)

anagram
A *word* or words that contains exactly the same letters but in a different order.
Examples: **pea**, **ape**; **fowl**, **flow**, **wolf**;
seaside, **disease**

base word
A *word* to which *prefixes* and *suffixes* can be added.
Example: **obey** (base word) + **dis** (prefix) =
disobey + **ed** (suffix) = **disobeyed**

comparative
An *adjective* that shows a degree of comparison between two or more things.
Examples: **big** (one), **bigger** (two), **biggest** (three or more); Jack is tall but Tom is taller.

compound word
A *word* made up of two or more smaller words, often developing first as a hyphenated word.
Examples: **butter** + **fly** = **butterfly**;
gold field, **gold-field**, **goldfield**

consonant
A letter in which the air is in some way impeded when pronounced. There are 21 consonants in the alphabet, all the letters that are not *vowels*.

consonant blend
When two or more *consonants* come together to blend a sound. Examples: **st ick**, **sk y**, **br own**, **str aw**
Consonant blends may be initial blends (**fr og**), medial (middle) blends (**blist er**), or final blends (**stamp**).

contraction
A *word* in which one or more letters have been omitted and in their place an apostrophe inserted.
Examples: **I would** becomes **I'd**;
is not becomes **isn't**

digraph
A combination of letters that represents a single sound. There are *consonant* digraphs and *vowel* digraphs. Common consonant digraphs include **sh**, **ch**, **th** and **wh**. (Consonant digraphs at the beginning of a word are called an onset.) A vowel digraph is called a *diphthong*.

homograph
A *word* that is spelled the same as another word, but each word has a different pronunciation and a different meaning.
Examples: **bear** (a furry animal) and **bear** (to carry); **palm** (a tree) and **palm** (a part of your hand)

homonym
A *word* that is spelled and/or pronounced the same as another word but each word has a different meaning. *Homographs* and *homophones* are both types of homonym, and some homonyms are both homographs and homophones. Examples: **tear** (rip) and **tear** (result of crying) **fair** (blond) and **fare** (cost of a train ticket) **bank** (place to exchange money) and **bank** (either side of a river)

homophone
A *word* that is pronounced the same as another word, but each word has a different spelling and a different meaning.
Examples: **bear** (a furry animal) and **bare** (naked)
sure (certain) and **shore** (coastline)

letter pattern
A letter sequence that functions as a unit and is related to a consistent category of sound.
Example: **one** = **bone**, **cone**, **tone**

long vowel
The sound of a *vowel* (**a**, **e**, **i**, **o**, **u**) that says its letter name, or is an *r-influenced vowel*.
Examples: **sa me**, **ba con**, **fa r**, **concre te**, **fe ver**, **fi ne**, **ri val**, **fi r**, **co ne**, **ro bot**, **co re**, **cu te**, **stu dent**, **pu rr**

noun
A *word* that refers to the names of everything around us.

phonics
The systematic relationship between letters and sounds.

plural
More than one. Most words make their plurals by adding an **s**. However, there are other ways to make the plurals of words.
Examples: **girl**, **girls**; **watch**, **watches**; **city**, **cities**; **piano**, **pianos**; **knife**, **knives**; **tooth**, **teeth**; **mouse**, **mice**

possessive
A *word* that shows that someone (or something) has ownership through the use of an apostrophe.
Example: **the boy's bike**; **the ladies' dresses**

prefix
Letters added to the beginning of a word, sometimes to make its opposite. We simply add these and no spelling changes to the base word are necessary.
Example: **in** + **visible** = **invisible**

r-influenced vowel
A vowel sound that is determined by the letter **r** following it. Example: the **a** in **far** is a *long vowel* sound but the **a** in **fad** is a *short vowel* sound.

root word
A *word* or word part that has its origin in Old English, Latin or Greek and that provides the basis of many other words.
Example: **aero** (air) = **aerial**, **aeroplane**, **aerobics**

short vowel
The sound of a *vowel* (**a**, **e**, **i**, **o** and **u**) that is clipped — a short sound. It is sometimes said short vowel sounds are the "baby" sounds.
Examples: **bat**, **bet**, **bit**, **bottle**, **but**

shortened word
A *word* that, over the years, has become shortened.
Example: **omnibus** (full version in use fifty or more years ago), **bus** (current usage)

silent (unsounded) letter
A letter in some words that is not pronounced but is still included in the word.
Examples: **lamb**, **know**, **pneumonia**, **sword**, **wrap**

suffix
A *word* ending that alters the word's part of speech (noun to adjective, for example) or meaning. Spelling changes are often needed.
Example: **beauty** + **ful** = **beautiful**

syllable
A sound unit that includes only one sounded *vowel*. The vowel may be preceded or followed by several *consonants*. Words can be divided into their syllables. This is a useful spelling technique.
Example: **development** = **de** / **vel** / **op** / **ment**

vowel
A letter in which the air passes through the mouth without obstruction when pronounced. The letters **a**, **e**, **i**, **o** and **u** are vowels. Note: **y** does the work of the vowels **i** and **e** in words such as **cry** (long **i**), **mystery** (short **i**) and **weary** (long **e**).

word
A unit of meaning. A word may be a simple *syllable* or a combination of syllables. A word may contain smaller units of meaning within it.

Answers, Class 4

Unit 1

A

1. bacon
2. waste
3. bracelet
4. fatal
5. lazy
6. vacant
7. escape
8. behave
9. crayons
10. crater

B

1. crane
2. chase
3. famous
4. whale
5. daisy
6. drake
7. blade
8. pirate
9. stables
10. rainbow

Unit 2

A

1. cactus
2. vanish
3. attic
4. camel
5. canvas
6. gallop
7. tablet
8. planet

B

1. hammer
2. traffic
3. palace
4. cabbage
5. tadpole
6. magic
7. wagon
8. chapter
9. nappy
10. lantern

C

Long a:
maybe
cable
layer
change
Short a:
habit
cabin
rapid
batter

Unit 3

A

1. female
2. even
3. evening
4. compete
5. complete
6. meter
7. here
8. fever
9. cedar
10. these

B

1. season
2. easy
3. trapeze
4. greedy
5. neon
6. asleep
7. peanut
8. neat
9. canteen
10. beetle

Unit 4

A

1. centre
2. cent
3. tennis
4. insect
5. pencil
6. sentence
7. pest
8. twenty
9. fence
10. letter

B

1. metal
2. level
3. denim
4. lemon
5. pedal
6. petal
7. medal
8. never
9. seven
10. melon

Unit 5

A

1. spider
2. describe
3. higher
4. blindfold
5. pirate
6. alive
7. driveway
8. iceberg
9. ninety
10. surprise

B

1. pilot
2. Friday
3. siren
4. tiger
5. silent
6. title
7. minus
8. rival
9. bridle
10. nightmare

Unit 6

A

1. pillows
2. city
3. kitten
4. lizard
5. chilly
6. slipper
7. skinny
8. winter
9. dinner

B

1. Yes
2. No
3. Yes
4. No
5. Yes
6. No
7. Yes
8. No
9. Yes
10. No

Unit 7 Revision

A

Long a:
stable
crayon
stage
behave
Short a:
apple
tadpole
wagon
cactus

B

Long e:
here
easy
complete
female
Short e:
pencil
tennis
cent
pest

C

Long i:
ninety
highest
hive
chime
Short i:
limb
twist
knit
comic

Unit 8 Test 1

1. stable
2. crayons
3. canvas
4. tadpoles
5. here
6. complete
7. cents
8. insect
9. surprise
10. pilot
11. lizard
12. winter

Unit 9 Test 2

1. cradle
2. famous
3. basket
4. magic
5. detour
6. easy
7. temper
8. welcome
9. kindness

10. brightly
11. river
12. picture

Unit 10

A

1. birds
2. apples
3. cows
4. books
5. chairs
6. weeds
7. pets
8. pencils

B

1. men
2. feet
3. women
4. mice
5. geese
6. children

Unit 11

A

1. watches
2. dishes
3. bunches
4. peaches
5. cockroaches
6. matches

B

1. buses
2. foxes
3. gases
4. guesses
5. boxes
6. glasses
7. dresses
8. hisses

Unit 12

1. toys
2. stories
3. babies
4. turkeys
5. cherries
6. flies
7. ladies
8. donkeys
9. keys
10. poppies

Unit 13

A

1. handcuffs
2. reefs
3. dwarfs
4. giraffes
5. cliffs
6. handkerchiefs
7. roofs
8. hoofs

B

1. loaves
2. knives
3. wolves
4. halves
5. scarves
6. leaves

Unit 14 Revision

A

+ s:
trolleys
pencils
donkeys
trees
papers
keys

+ es:
buses
peaches
dresses
matches
foxes
wishes

Change y to i + es:
ladies
lollies
flies
poppies
diaries
cities

B

1. wishes
2. buses
3. matches
4. turkeys
5. cities
6. teeth
7. women
8. mice

Unit 15 Test

1. gases
2. dresses
3. donkeys
4. parrots
5. peaches
6. fairies
7. glasses
8. giraffes
9. knives
10. lollies
11. branches
12. flies

Unit 16

A

1. ladybird
2. goldfish
3. crossroad
4. armchair
5. eyebrow
6. horseshoe
7. seagull
8. lighthouse

B

1. tugboat
2. sunlight
3. strawberry
4. necklace
5. rainbow
6. broomstick
7. campfire
8. tablecloth
9. waterfall

Unit 17

A

1. toothpaste
2. windmill
3. football
4. overcoat
5. starfish
6. spaceship
7. grasshopper
8. freeway

B

1. blacksmith, blackbird, blackberry
2. bedroom, bedspread, bedtime
3. lifeboat, lifejacket, lifetime
4. raincoat, raindrop, rainfall
5. eyelash, eyelid, eyeball
6. homesick, homemade, homework
7. birthday, birthmark, birthstone
8. horseshoe, horseback, horsepower

Unit 18

1. bandage
2. wagon
3. missile
4. telescope
5. altar
6. dentist
7. aquarium
8. pedestrian

Unit 19

A

1. ocean
2. poem
3. pony
4. hoping
5. grocery
6. froze
7. toe
8. sofa
9. stone
10. doze

B

1. rope
2. rose
3. nose
4. home
5. cone
6. alone
7. explode
8. hotel
9. bone
10. telephone

Unit 20

A

1. comet
2. follow
3. cottage
4. popcorn
5. doctor
6. honest
7. cotton
8. bottle
9. blossom
10. foggy

B

1. Yes
2. No
3. Yes
4. Yes
5. No
6. No
7. Yes
8. No

9. Yes
10. No

Unit 21

A

1. excuse
2. beautiful
3. pupil
4. student
5. cubes
6. fumes
7. pure
8. music
9. fuse
10. mule

B

1. tulip
2. cute
3. tuna
4. reduce
5. bugle
6. student
7. perfume
8. puny
9. computer
10. stupid

Unit 22

A

1. thunder
2. funny
3. umpire
4. supper
5. butter
6. puppet
7. tunnel
8. hungry
9. trumpet
10. bucket

B

1. hump
2. lunch
3. uncle
4. ugly
5. crust
6. skull
7. bunk
8. truck
9. plum
10. bunch

Unit 23

A

1. shark
2. March
3. cartoons
4. garden
5. starve
6. target
7. smart
8. harvest
9. alarm
10. parcel

B

1. store
2. forty
3. corner
4. storm
5. thorn
6. shore
7. story
8. torch
9. torn
10. short

Unit 24

A

1. newspaper
2. whisper
3. tiger
4. timber
5. silver
6. spider

B

1. skirt
2. chirp
3. smirk
4. birthday
5. squirt
6. circus
7. circle
8. stir

C

1. burst
2. sunburned
3. urn
4. nurse

Unit 25 Revision

A

Long o sound:
ocean
cone
explode
pony
Short o sound:
cottage
doctor
cotton
comet

B

Long u sound:
tulip
bugle
music
cube
Short u sound:
bunch
bucket
skull
truck

C

ar: sound
barge
carton
or sound:
forty
thorn
er sound:
ladder
spider
ir = er sound:
circle
shirt
ur = er sound:
turkey
burst

Unit 26 Test 1

1. ocean
2. telephone
3. follow
4. cotton
5. excuse
6. student
7. bucket
8. puppet
9. turn
10. garden
11. silver
12. thirsty

Unit 27 Test 2

1. hoping
2. alone
3. doctor
4. bottle
5. excuse
6. student
7. funny
8. crust
9. shark
10. corner
11. stir
12. suburb

Unit 28

A

1. looked
2. showed
3. played
4. landed
5. rushed
6. watched
7. asked
8. stayed
9. visited
10. minded

B

1. sweeping
2. washing
3. cooking
4. climbing
5. brushing
6. drinking

Unit 29

A

1. hopped
2. chopped
3. stopped
4. dragged
5. rubbed
6. clapped
7. flipped
8. clipped
9. strapped
10. gripped

B

1. swimming
2. shopping
3. running
4. hitting
5. cutting
6. swapping

Unit 30

A

1. chased
2. saved
3. changed
4. baked
5. waved
6. placed
7. raced
8. dived
9. hoped
10. faced

B

1. riding
2. skating
3. biting

4. making
5. driving
6. hiding

Unit 31

A

1. bat
2. wash
3. pick
4. row
5. lift
6. ask
7. pull
8. cover
9. bark
10. kick

B

1. drag
2. chop
3. rub
4. stop
5. drop
6. shop
7. net
8. call
9. grip
10. strap

C

1. clapped
2. slapped
3. dripped

Unit 32 Revision

A

No change:
played
helped
kicked
filled
growled
washed
cooked
planted
Double last letter:
stepped
dragged
shopped
skipped
clapped
chopped
mopped
hopped

B

No change:
blocking
helping
growling
cooking
Double last letter:
running
skipping
mopping
stepping
Drop e:
skating
hiking
riding
moving

Unit 33 Test

1. helped
2. skipping
3. picked
4. riding
5. shopping
6. swimming
7. drinking
8. blocked
9. asked
10. trotted
11. scrubbing
12. racing

Unit 34

A

1. sail
2. creek
3. toe
4. eight
5. flower
6. rain
7. knot
8. plane

B

1. sum, some
2. ring, wring
3. hole, whole
4. rose, rows
5. hour, our
6. toe, tow
7. roar, raw
8. blue, blew

C

1. pear
2. rose
3. sum

Unit 35

A

1. steak
2. tied
3. week
4. stare
5. cheap
6. tide
7. stake
8. weak
9. stair
10. cheep

B

1. eight
2. plane
3. bean
4. rain
5. pear
6. mail
7. road
8. horse

Unit 36

A

1. Spaghetti: from an Italian word meaning string.
2. Corn: from an Old English word meaning wordn-down particle.
3. Date: from a Latin word meaning finger.
4. Lettuce: from a Latin word meaning milk-giving plant.
5. Cabbage: from a Latin word meaning head.
6. Onlelette: from a French word meaning thin blade of a sword.

Unit 37

A

1. bawl
2. straw
3. yawn
4. hawk
5. lawn
6. jaw
7. dawn
8. awful
9. crawl
10. drawn

B

1. Yes
2. No
3. Yes
4. No
5. Yes
6. Yes
7. No
8. Yes

Unit 38

A

1. steel
2. fleet
3. kneel
4. creek
5. queen
6. cheese
7. sweet
8. asleep
9. fifteen
10. wheels

B

1. hooves
2. snooze
3. school
4. rooster
5. cocoon
6. tooth
7. goose
8. hoop

Unit 39

A

1. boast
2. toast
3. throat
4. toad
5. cloak
6. soak
7. moat
8. loaves
9. coach
10. cocoa

B

1. noise
2. loyal
3. poison
4. voice
5. annoy
6. joint
7. enjoy
8. choice
9. moist
10. spoiled

Unit 40

A

1. snail
2. daisy
3. chain
4. grain
5. straight
6. sailor

7. drains
8. afraid
9. paint
10. train

B

1. fried
2. grief
3. niece
4. died
5. cried
6. dried
7. brief
8. thief

Unit 41

A

1. wheat
2. peach
3. leaf
4. beam
5. steal
6. clean
7. cream
8. beach
9. leap
10. stream

B

1. meant
2. breath
3. instead
4. heavy
5. bread
6. feathers
7. head
8. leather
9. ready
10. weather

Unit 42

A

1. towel
2. crowd
3. clown
4. crown
5. powder
6. shower
7. brown
8. allow
9. tower
10. flower

B

1. mower
2. yellow
3. shadow
4. pillow
5. arrow
6. snowing
7. shallow
8. elbow
9. hollow
10. window

Unit 43 Revision

A

1. daughter
2. dawn
3. saucer
4. hawk
5. lawn
6. naughty
7. bawl
8. sauce

B

1. snooze
2. fleet
3. fifteen
4. rooster
5. kneel
6. goose
7. creek
8. school

C

1. loaf
2. moist
3. toast
4. joint
5. coast
6. poison
7. spoiled
8. toad

D

ea = long e sound:
stream
cream
beach
steal

ea = short e sound:
feather
ready
breath
bread

Unit 44 Test 1

1. jaw
2. daughter
3. dawn
4. sauce
5. queen
6. wheel
7. snooze
8. rooster
9. boat
10. toast
11. poison
12. voice

Unit 45 Test 2

1. crawl
2. wheat
3. cheese
4. school
5. boast
6. choice
7. tower
8. meant
9. drain
10. brief
11. clean
12. heavy

Unit 46

A

1. feel
2. weep
3. help
4. pick
5. weed
6. climb
7. drink
8. ask
9. pull
10. row

B

1. clap
2. mop
3. skip
4. swim
5. chop
6. run
7. put
8. shop
9. plan
10. dig

C

1. like
2. tame
3. hike
4. move
5. taste
6. race
7. skate
8. ride
9. shape
10. bake

Unit 47

A

1. brightly
2. quickly
3. bravely
4. loudly
5. slowly
6. badly
7. sweetly
8. proudly
9. safely
10. cleverly

B

1. comfortably
2. heavily
3. angrily
4. hungrily
5. noisily
6. gently
7. easily
8. truly
9. terribly
10. possibly

Unit 48

A

1. seven
2. ribbon
3. cousin
4. fountain
5. cotton
6. pumpkin
7. broken
8. napkin
9. mountain

B

1. gravel
2. camel
3. travel
4. middle
5. table
6. kettle
7. bottle
8. little
9. turtle

Unit 49

A

1. sailor
2. anchor
3. mirror
4. ladder
5. freezer

6. dollar
7. burglar
8. tractor

B

1. collar
2. faster
3. blister
4. cellar
5. solar
6. author
7. doctor
8. mayor
9. speaker
10. jogger

Unit 50 Revision

A

+ ar:
lunar
solar
dollar
collar
beggar
regular
+ er:
timber
ladder
freezer
proper
skater
dreamer
+ or:
mayor
anchor
tractor
motor
author
mirror

B

+ en:
eleven
heaven
children
broken
+ in:
cabin
cousin
napkin
pumpkin
+ on:
apron
ribbon
dragon
cotton
+ ain:
captain
curtain
fountain
mountain

Unit 51 Test

1. bottle
2. broken
3. angrily
4. gently
5. taming
6. hiking
7. safely
8. travel
9. cotton
10. mountain
11. tractor
12. turtle

Unit 52

A

1. rock
2. bear
3. mine
4. light
5. train
6. rock
7. bear
8. train
9. mine
10. light

B

1. a creek bank
2. a fence post
3. the bark of a dog
4. a storage box
5. a ball for sport
6. a cricket bat

Unit 53

A

1. plum
2. wand
3. meal
4. bear
5. ring
6. wolf
7. shoe
8. pear

B

1. clean
2. rose
3. bowl
4. shoe
5. star
6. vase

Unit 54

1. fence
2. pram
3. taxi
4. flu
5. wig
6. bus
7. zoo
8. Halloween

Unit 55

A

1. found
2. hound
3. south
4. ground
5. pouch
6. outside
7. thousand
8. around
9. flour
10. proud

B

1. Yes
2. No
3. No
4. Yes
5. No
6. Yes

Unit 56

A

1. cheese
2. chicken
3. child
4. cheap
5. chess
6. cherry
7. chief
8. chase
9. chapter
10. chest

B

1. shrub
2. shoulder
3. shrimp
4. shadow
5. shiny
6. shatter
7. shovel
8. shampoo
9. shoe
10. shrink

Unit 57

A

1. thirteen
2. threw
3. thumb
4. thongs
5. thunder
6. thorn
7. thrush
8. throat
9. Thursday
10. throne

B

1. Yes
2. Yes
3. No
4. No
5. Yes
6. Yes

Unit 58

A

1. chicken
2. quack
3. thick
4. bucket
5. black
6. cricket
7. stick
8. brick
9. flock
10. packet

B

1. quarrel
2. quail
3. queen
4. queer
5. quadrangle
6. quilt
7. quarry
8. quartz
9. quince
10. quartet

Unit 59

A

1. dragon
2. crayon
3. breakfast
4. clam
5. planet
6. grape
7. freckle
8. flour

B

1. spider
2. scream
3. prune
4. snooze
5. skinny
6. scone

C

1. tusk
2. guest
3. grunt
4. eucalypt
5. hound
6. stamp
7. lung
8. adult

Unit 60

A

1. school
2. hour
3. knife
4. knee
5. wrist
6. crumb
7. limb
8. sword
9. palm
10. calf

B

ghost (h)
answer (w)
kneel (k)
honest (h)
castle (t)
sign (g)
half (l)
bomb (b)

Unit 61 Revision

A

ou = ow sound:
bound
around
south
hound

ou = long oo sound:
soup
you
group
cantaloupe

ou = short u sound:
country
double
touch
rough

B

1. shampoo
2. cherry
3. shrub
4. chicken
5. shadow
6. shriek
7. chocolate
8. chisel

C

1. wheat
2. thirty
3. white
4. thirsty
5. thumb
6. whale
7. whisper
8. thief

Unit 62 Test 1

1. touch
2. pouch
3. soup
4. shallow
5. chief
6. thumb
7. wheeze
8. bucket
9. quacked
10. freckles
11. guest
12. skinny

Unit 63 Test 2

1. flour
2. rough
3. shampoo
4. chemist
5. quarrel
6. packet
7. blanket
8. swallow
9. glutton
10. slippers
11. school
12. basket

Unit 64

A

1. older
2. smoother
3. slower
4. lighter
5. faster
6. cooler
7. cleaner
8. stronger
9. sweeter
10. younger

B

1. oldest
2. cleanest
3. brightest
4. steepest
5. slowest
6. youngest
7. smartest
8. coolest

Unit 65

A

1. busier
2. heavier
3. tinier
4. noisier
5. healthier
6. bigger
7. redder
8. hotter
9. fatter
10. thinner

B

1. prettiest
2. busiest
3. luckiest
4. heaviest
5. wealthiest
6. hottest
7. fattest
8. maddest
9. saddest
10. fittest

Unit 66

A

1. misbehave
2. repay
3. uncomfortable
4. inexpensive
5. insensitive
6. return
7. unreliable
8. mistake

B

1. bicycle
2. quartet
3. binoculars
4. semicircle
5. unicycle
6. tricycle
7. octopus
8. triangle

Unit 67

A

1. the girl's dress
2. the teacher's car
3. the book's pages
4. the wolf's howl
5. the lady's television
6. the chair's legs

B

1. the dogs' tails
2. the horses' manes
3. the houses' roofs
4. the boys' bikes
5. the ladies' dresses
6. the trees' trunks
7. the teachers' pens
8. the clocks' hands

Unit 68 Revision

1. slower, slowest
2. cooler, coolest
3. cleaner, cleanest
4. younger, youngest
5. faster, fastest
6. olde, oldest
7. steeper, steepest
8. smoother, smoothest

B

1. busier, busiest
2. prettier, prettiest
3. muddier, muddiest
4. dizzier, dizziest
5. heavier, heaviest
6. tinier, tiniest
7. noisier, noisiest
8. fussier, fussiest

C

Sam's bicycle
man's dog
cities' towers
dog's collar
mouse's squeaks
ladies' dresses
trees' leaves
teacher's car

Unit 69 Test

1. hotter
2. busier
3. slower
4. tiniest
5. luckier
6. redder
7. saddest
8. tricycle
9. octopus

10. rewrite
11. unreliable
12. invisible

Unit 70

A

1. they are
2. she will
3. I will
4. I would
5. is not
6. you would
7. we would
8. she is
9. have not
10. can not
11. did not
12. who is

B

1. they're
2. we've
3. won't
4. you've
5. I'm
6. can't
7. doesn't

Unit 71

1. meter
2. loose
3. quite
4. drawers
5. except
6. breathe
7. too
8. there
9. allowed
10. knew
11. rowed
12. they're
13. off
14. adopt

Unit 72

A

1. nice thought
2. refined, knowledgeable
3. bad, no good
4. act out, to be funny
5. squeezed up

B

1. annoys
2. strange, odd
3. playing up, being silly
4. saveloy in a bread roll
5. large machine

Unit 73

A

1. fried (ie)
2. towel (ow)
3. moist (oi)
4. cried (ie)
5. toast (oa)
6. mower (ow)
7. toad (oa)
8. spoiled (oi)
9. poison (oi)
10. niece (ie)
11. crown (ow)
12. shallow (ow)
13. loaf (oa)
14. brief (ie)
15. coat (oa)
16. joint (oi)

B

1. birthday
2. tiger
3. circus
4. thorn
5. yesterday
6. store
7. shore
8. forty
9. thirsty
10. ladder

Unit 74 Test 1

1. foxes
2. geese
3. dresses
4. donkeys
5. halves
6. giraffes
7. flies
8. ladies
9. churches
10. berries
11. gases
12. books

Unit 75 Test 2

1. racing
2. moving
3. swimming
4. planning
5. easily
6. truly
7. safely
8. broken
9. gravel
10. ribbon
11. anchor
12. tractor

Unit 76 Test 3

1. telephone
2. motel
3. tulip
4. music
5. bugle
6. bottle
7. camel
8. puppet
9. garden
10. daisies
11. feathers
12. cotton